Partner
BETRAYAL TRAUMA

DOUGLAS WEISS, PH.D.

Partner Betrayal Trauma

Requests for information:
Discovery Press
heart2heart@xc.org
719-278-3708

Printed in the United States of America
ISBN # 978-1-881292-42-5

Cover and Interior Design by Janelle Evangelides

Table of Contents

Introduction

Every book has a story. Let me tell you my story as a leader in the Partner Movement, giving a voice to partners of betrayal trauma.

In the early 1980s, there was a huge recovery awakening (not just alcohol and drugs), but codependency, sex addiction, and food addiction. The process addiction movement was different than drugs and alcohol addiction because chemicals aren't involved.

Sex addiction started in the height of the codependency movement. Patrick Carnes wrote the first book on sex addiction called *Out of the Shadows* (1983). Dr. Carnes' research was groundbreaking for sex addiction and he introduced the co-addict model for partners of sex addicts. The core beliefs of a co-addict are:

1. I am a bad and unworthy person
2. No one would love me as I am
3. My needs are never going to be met
4. Sex is the most important sign of love

This is where I come in. In 1993, I wrote the book *Women Who Love Sex Addicts* (one of only a few books for spouses of sex addicts). This book provided validation of trauma betrayal, grief, and anger that a partner of a sex addict goes through and how to recover. Since the prevailing model 26 years ago used the co-addict language for partners of sex addicts, this book contained that language.

However, since my first year as a clinician (and almost daily counseling partners of sex addicts), the co-addict model just wasn't working for me. I was counseling women married to sex addicts, but they were strong, smart, and attractive. They were also spiritually, emotionally, and sexually mature. I kept thinking there has to be a better term for women married to, or in a significant relationship with, a sex addict.

Therefore, I created the Partner Movement and renamed these women "partners" instead of "co-addicts." In 2001, I wrote the books, *Partners: Healing from His Addiction*, as well as the *Partners Recovery* Guide, and *Beyond Love: A 12- Step Guide for Partners of Sex Addicts.* These resources give dignity back to the courageous women who happen to marry sex addicts.

In the *Partners* book, I begin to outline the impact from the trauma of living with a sex addict. In the workbooks, I empower partners to heal.

As the President of the American Association for Sex Addiction Therapy (AASAT), we produced the first certification to treat partners of sex addicts. The principles of the Partner Movement that we have utilized for more than 30 years are:

1. Every partner is absolutely unique and worthy of honor for whom they presently are.

2. The partner has no responsibility for the addict's addiction or acting out.

3. Partners come from anywhere on the continuum of spiritual, emotional, physical, financial, sexual, and social health.

4. Any partner who takes responsibility for herself can heal and grow in areas she deems necessary.

5. The addiction often creates collateral damage that is best to heal from as early as possible.

6. There are no core beliefs or attributes for partners. They are all unique beings.

As in any healthy movement or family, voices with influence need to be heard and validated. In 2009, Barbara Steffens and Marsha Means wrote the book *Your Sexually Addicted Spouse: How Partners Can Cope and Heal.* The authors highlight from a post-traumatic stress model that some partners experience the betrayal involved in sex addiction like post-traumatic stress. They brought the terms "trigger" and "gaslighting" to the movement.

In the partner camp another voice emerged from Jennifer Freyd's work on sexual abuse. Dr. Freyd brings two important insights to the Partner Movement. First, the level of intimacy between partner and addict determines the level of partner trauma. For example, a father sexually abusing his daughter is different than a stranger. Second, because of the need to survive, the child will have to minimize, suppress, and cope with the trauma to survive within the father-daughter relationship.

Let me validate the voices of partners when it comes to sex addiction, infidelity, and intimacy anorexia—partner betrayal trauma is absolutely real. I have been working with partner betrayal trauma for over 30 years. I've seen women like you convulse, retch, scream like animals, go blank, tremble, and yell "No, No" over and over again as they hear the truth of how their husband betrayed them. I get it. Prior to marriage, I lived with a woman who cheated on me and it ripped my young heart to pieces.

The interdependence in marriage is a real dynamic, and a woman's circumstances as well as economic or emotional dependence, can all be factors in her partner recovery process.

As a father in this movement, I welcome all the voices of partner recovery. This is not an either/or discussion but a both/and for partners and their recovery choices. Not all partners are alike. Not all sex abuse survivors react to the same recovery process as others. Most partners do well in the general recovery process for partners of sex addicts. Others benefit greatly from some of the PTSD or betrayal information.

I believe as a Partner Movement we can learn and love each other as we continue to grow. My heart is that we respect and grow together.

This book is a validation of what I have been talking about, defending and treating partners of sex addicts. This book looks at betrayal, something partners of sex addicts, infidelity survivors, and spouses of intimacy anorexics will need to address.

This book is based upon research (not whims, theories, or biases from other theories). In 2018, we conducted a research study of 154 women who have experienced betrayal trauma. These women were asked to complete a 2-hour questionnaire with valid measures to assess the Partner Betrayal Model. Interestingly, regardless if the trauma came through infidelity, sex addiction, or intimacy anorexia, there were no statistically significant differences in the study. Therefore, the study reveals the outcome wasn't about what happened to the partner, but who did it. The husband or significant other betrayed her and that is what causes trauma.

As women work through the betrayal, and embark on the journey of partner recovery, they can be the amazing person they were meant to be. I have seen thousands of women heal and become stronger as a result of this process. This book is dedicated to your courageous journey.

1

Trusted

"Dr. Weiss, why do I hurt so badly? It feels like all of me hurts inside and out." I have heard this question thousands of times in my 30+ years of caring for partners of betrayal trauma. These women come from every walk of life—every color, every age, every religion, and on every continent.

A partner is smart, attractive, intelligent, good hearted, faithful to her husband, and she is writhing in pain because she has been betrayed. She has tears in her eyes and stains on her face from the tears she has shedded as she asks again, "Why do I hurt so badly?"

When she has had enough time to feel this, she looks at me again with a look of "Okay, I'm back. Talk to me." I tell her, "The reason you hurt so much is because you love so much." She nods her head in acknowledgement. That is exactly why she hurts so badly.

Let me share with you how I explain the trauma of betrayal to her in a very practical way.

Mary Jo is an executive with an MBA. She makes over six figures, is successful, athletic, a faithful wife, and mother of two daughters. Her husband is also a professional and travels. Unbeknownst to Mary Jo, her husband was addicted to porn his entire life. Over the last five years when her husband traveled, his behavior shifted to prostitutes and one-night stands. Mary Jo was informed of all of this when her husband was told he would lose his job if he didn't get "significant help." The couple came to my office to do an Intensive. Her husband completed a polygraph clarifying the extent of his behavior.

Even though Mary Jo already knew 90% of what was on the polygraph, she was still in pain from all the betrayal from her husband of 14 years. She couldn't understand why she was hurting so badly.

I said, "Mary Jo I want you to stand up. I want you to lean all of your body weight on this chair." She did. "Now in this position you're all in in trusting. You have no defense, no balance, no safety. This is the position you were in when your husband sucker punched you with his betrayal of you. You had no defense against this hit at all. That's why you hurt all over. The trauma cracks from his betrayal have gone through all aspects of your being (spiritually, emotionally, cognitively, and sexually) but also to other areas of your life. You're feeling multiple fractures and the multi-dimensional impact of betrayal trauma.

I encourage you to find a stable sofa or chair, and lean all in. Let your body and soul totally trust the chair. This is who you are. You are all in; all trusting, all giving, and a faithful, amazing woman.

That is why I started this book with a chapter on trust. It's because you have fully trusted in the past that you are now experiencing trauma from the betrayal. The reason that your pain is so great is because you were vulnerable and all in.

"THE REASON THAT YOUR PAIN IS SO GREAT IS BECAUSE YOU WERE VULNERABLE AND ALL IN."

In this first chapter, I want to highlight many ways you probably trusted your husband before the betrayal. The partner betrayal trauma story doesn't start when a woman finds out about the betrayal. It starts when her heart is all in the relationship with the man who betrayed her.

There were many days you gave your heart, trust, and sexuality to this man you loved. You dated and bought wholeheartedly the image of him that he was creating for you.

Then came the day you put on your white dress and walked down the aisle to the classic tune of "Here Comes the Bride." You declared before God, family, and friends, you were all in with this man. You heard him declare some version that he would "forsake all others and love, honor and cherish you."

You trusted him. You trusted him as you moved into apartments and houses, bought furniture, dreamed together, and as you supported him in his career. You trusted him to have children together, including all of the joys and responsibilities that come with it.

When you go back through the movie of your life, do you see that you were all in, with this man? You trusted, and this trusting is where the story begins.

Your trust has been impacted significantly due to his betrayal. His betrayal is huge because the marriage relationship is so intertwined. The Bible says when we get married "The two will become one flesh" (Genesis 2). This is probably the best word picture ever written about marriage.

You become one unit. This marriage combines and utilizes your various strengths and weaknesses. You extended your trust to him in the most significant manner humanly possible.

This is the entire argument for partner betrayal trauma. The sacred, multi-dimensional, interdependent relationship of marriage is a totally different, unique, and much more intimate relationship, than any other relationship possible.

The marriage relationship has trust as one of its key ingredients to be successful. I know I can totally trust my wife Lisa in every area of our lives, and she knows she can trust me. This trust helps us stay intimate as friends and lovers, but also practically it allows us to function seamlessly on so many personal and professional areas of our lives.

Trust is a very powerful gift you give someone. Total trust (spirit, soul, body, sexual, and financial) is the kind of trust you give to the one man you are all in with. You trusted him in so many areas of your life.

Your trust was huge before betrayal and became part of your story due to no fault of your own. He chose to betray you, whether with porn or sex with others (known or unknown to you), or through intimacy anorexia and withholding himself from you. Regardless if you're a partner because of sex addiction, infidelity, or intimacy anorexia you are a partner who has experienced betrayal and the trauma that comes with that betrayal.

Here I will highlight how multifaceted your trust has been of your husband or significant other. I also want to validate that you trusted him before you knew. Remember that some of you had a "knowing" that something was wrong before you had the facts.

A total of 151 women completed the *Weiss Relationship Trust Questionnaire.* These women were asked to rate the amount of trust they experienced toward their spouse or significant other "before" and "after" betrayal. In Chapter Three (Betrayed) I will go into more detail from each of the specific areas and compare "before" betrayal scores with "after" betrayal scores.

The *Weiss Relationship Trust Questionnaire* is organized using a 5-point Likert scale with 1 = No Trust (*Not at All*) and 5 = High Trust (*Totally*). The first set of questions relate to trust before finding out about the betrayal from your husband or significant other. Women were asked about trust in the following areas:

Overall Trust
Emotionally
Spiritually
Socially
Sexually
Financially
Parenting
General responsibilities
Extended family relationships
Keeping their word
Follow through with their commitments

Prior to your knowledge of betrayal, did you trust your husband/significant other?

1. 5%   2. 8%   3. 9%   4. 27%   5. 51%

Prior to your knowledge of betrayal, did you trust your husband/significant other emotionally?

1. 8%   2. 10%   3. 17%   4. 27%   5. 38%

Prior to your knowledge of betrayal, did you trust your husband/significant other spiritually?

1. 12%   2. 15%   3. 16%   4. 25%   5. 32%

Prior to your knowledge of betrayal, did you trust your husband/significant other in social situations?

1. 7%   2. 12%   3. 20%   4. 23%   5. 38%

Prior to your knowledge of betrayal, did you trust your husband/significant other sexually?

1. 6%   2. 14%   3. 11%   4. 26%   5. 43%

Prior to your knowledge of betrayal, did you trust your husband/significant other financially?

1. 10%   2. 12%   3. 14%   4. 27%   5. 37%

Prior to your knowledge of betrayal, did you trust your husband's/significant other's parenting?

1. 5%   2. 19%   3. 31%   4. 23%   5. 22%

Prior to your knowledge of betrayal, did you trust your husband/significant other with general responsibilities?

1. 5%   2. 14%   3. 23%   4. 31%   5. 27%

Prior to your knowledge of betrayal, did you trust your husband/significant other in other extended family relationships?

1. 6%   2. 16%   3. 21%   4. 24%   5. 33%

Prior to your knowledge of betrayal, did you trust your husband/significant other to keep their word?

1. 9%   2. 12%   3. 21%   4. 29%   5. 29%

Prior to your knowledge of betrayal, did you trust your husband/significant other to follow through with their commitments?

1. 10%   2. 14%   3. 19%   4. 29%   5. 29%

These results show that overall you trusted your husband or significant other in various areas of your life. After betrayal (as we will see in Chapter Three) there is a significant impact in your ability to trust. This is normal. However, trust can be restored if he works his recovery, and you decide to give trust (more on this later).

So, now you understand how your trust has been impacted. But you still may not understand how he could do such a thing and this feeling sometimes goes on for years, or decades. "It still hurts!"

Yes, it still hurts but let me take you on another aspect as to why this hurts so much and why you still don't understand. The DVD *Unstuck*, was produced for partners who are stuck, (unable to move forward because they simply cannot understand his bad choices). In this resource, I explain the reason you are stuck is because you make good choices. The better the choices you make, the more stuck you can become from trying to understand the insane choices he has made in your life.

Let me explain this further (try to be patient with me through the end of this chapter). In my 30+ years of counseling sex addicts, intimacy anorexics, cheaters, and their partners, I discovered that people have two operating systems. These operating systems are completely opposite from each other and neither system understands that the other exists. The path then is to accept the other operating system, even if you don't understand it.

Let me explain. Some people live in "relational reality"

which is operating system #1. A person who lives in relational reality believes these core things:

1. People have value.

2. You should never lie, cheat, or steal.

3. There are consequences for bad choices for everyone.

When you live in relational reality much of the pain, suffering, and craziness of the world does not make sense to you.

However, there is also a totally different operating system in people around you.

When a soul is treated like an object, through neglect, abuse, abandonment, experiencing tragedy, or sexual abuse, this person has to learn to survive. To survive, this person may choose operating system #2 which is called "object reality." Through this process the person fully embraces these set of values:

1. People do not have value.

2. Lying, cheating, and stealing are acceptable.

3. There are no rules, or I can change them when I want to, and there are no consequences for me.

This soul is literally playing a video game of survival, not living. They see people as objects to manipulate for their safety (intimacy anorexic), or their benefit (addict). The addict, who suspends development when the addiction plays his nurse to get him through life, is stunted. Surviving is the option for the addict and the object relationship operating system is how they function.

You see because you are "good" you can't understand the

object relationship way of living. You try to make his sex with others about "loving or caring" about the other person, when the truth is that they simply were using them.

Your goodness only has the relational processor, so you will give relational meaning to a behavior of his that was not relational, but an object to him.

There is so much more here to say. That is why in the *Partner Betrayal Trauma Step Guide* address powerlessness. You can accept his object processing, even if you never understand it.

You partner betrayal trauma started way before your discovery day of his betrayal. Your betrayal started as you trusted and were an all in good woman. This is the context in which your betrayal occurred.

> "YOUR PARTNER BETRAYAL TRAUMA STARTED WAY BEFORE YOUR DISCOVERY DAY OF HIS BETRAYAL."

2

Discovery Day

Discovery day is by far the worst day of a woman's life. It was on this day you began to discover his secret life. This is the day that changed your life as you previously knew it.

Just today, I did a Q&A Facebook Live event for our Women's Partner Facebook Group (https://www.facebook.com/groups/partnersofsa/). One of the members asked this question, "Dr. Weiss, I have been married for almost forty years. I just found out about his cheating and his sex addiction which started all the way back to the beginning of our marriage. How do I try to put our past life together, love in the present, and even think of a future together?"

This question is very real for every partner of betrayal, whether it is infidelity, sex addiction, or intimacy anorexia. Every woman's journey, as they navigate these waters, is unique to them. The uniqueness of the quality of your marriage, his getting caught or disclosing voluntarily, his coming totally clean or dribbling disclosure, his response to heal or not heal, your trauma history, your resiliency factors, her economic situation and her own narrative, are all contributing factors on discovery day. That is why your discovery day, or multiple discovery days will be unique to you.

I have sat through many discovery days in my office when a woman receives the truth of his infidelity, sex addiction, or intimacy anorexia. The screaming, crying, yelling, and going blank are indelibly written on my heart and mind as I see her receiving the news of betrayal.

In this chapter, I want to highlight several factors that make this day different for everyone. You will have your own experience. I have literally heard and been a part of thousands of discovery days. I want to share these variables with you because they can help validate your experience, help you understand yourself, and help you understand the recovery of other partners of betrayal.

Quality of Marriage

Discovery of betrayal happens in a relational context. Betrayal can only happen if there is a relationship. The relationship (if it is healthy), supplies nutrition to both individuals and fortifies them against the impact of life's painful events. The healthier the marriage or relationship, the more fortified the soul, spirit, and body are to manage the trauma life can bring.

However, if the relationship is not healthy, it causes frustration and can drain her of the valid nutrition she needs in order to go through trauma. It may also exacerbate the impact of the trauma on her.

This is why understanding about intimacy anorexia (www.intimacyanorexia.com) can be very important to understand your situation. The following behaviors of an intimacy anorexic demonstrate areas of neglect in your marriage:

1. He is too busy for you
2. He blames you if a problem arises
3. He withholds love
4. He withholds praise
5. He withholds spiritually
6. He withholds sex, or is disengaged during sex
7. He uses anger or silence to control you
8. He is unwilling or unable to share his feelings with you
9. He has ongoing, or ungrounded criticism of you, whether he speaks it or not
10. He controls or shames around money issues
11. It feels like you are roommates, or you feel married and alone

If your husband (or you) have five or more of these behaviors, then intimacy anorexia is present. If he is an intimacy anorexic then the impact of trauma for you will be significantly increased. This will also impact your motivation to work on your marriage, since this relationship has not felt like a marriage most of the years you have been together.

Now in a healthy marriage you feel like friends, you feel like you are on a team together, you can share feelings, dreams, and responsibilities. You go on dates; sex is consistent and connecting. You feel loved by this man on a regular basis. You feel married because you are married.

In an unhealthy marriage, you feel like you're functioning, but not in a relationship. You feel alone and feelings are not shared. Dates are rare. Sex is one-sided (if it is happening), sex is less often, or less satisfying. You don't feel loved or cherished. The dryness of your marriage has become a dryness in your soul.

The quality of marriage is the context in which the photograph of discovery has been placed. You're aware of the quality of your marriage prior to discovery and your quality of marriage is uniquely yours.

Caught or Disclosing

For decades, every Monday morning when I do Five-Day Intensives with couples dealing with sex addiction, infidelity, and or intimacy anorexia, I ask specific questions. "Has there been porn, masturbation, or sex with others?" Usually the partner's answer is "Yes." Then I ask a very important question looking directly at the husband, "Were you caught, or did you voluntarily disclose?"

I am amazed at how often the husband initially says he disclosed, and then half of the time the story of him being caught eventually comes out. So, let me quickly share the difference between disclosing, versus getting caught.

Disclosing is when a man is so sick and tired of the double life that he knows he needs to stop. He knows he needs to tell his wife and has a sense of conviction that this is his only hope to heal. Then he picks a time and location to disclose the history of when it started, and the behaviors of his acting out.

For it to be "disclosure," it would 100% be from his intentional conviction to change, heal, or stop his secret lifestyle. This means he didn't lose his job and has to tell you why. This would rule out pressure from the affair partner, a stripper who is threatening to contact you, or some other external event like an STD, or a pregnancy motivating him to be honest.

Getting caught has happened in so many ways it could be its own book. Examples include the other person telling you, a friend seeing them together, the strip club secret, the condom or Viagra, the porn stash or website found, emails or texts, and what I call acts of God (something really bizarre happened to expose the behavior or put you on a path of discovering yourself). Sadly, sometimes the children find information that starts the disclosure.

The reason getting caught, or a self-motivated disclosure is important, is because it gives more context to how your betrayal information was brought to you. Having a husband sobbing about what he has done and how he hurt you and doesn't deserve you, is a totally different experience than many other women have.

"THE REASON GETTING CAUGHT, OR A SELF-MOTIVATED DISCLOSURE IS IMPORTANT, IS BECAUSE IT GIVES MORE CONTEXT TO HOW YOUR BETRAYAL INFORMATION WAS BROUGHT TO YOU."

The husband who is caught will minimize, lie, answer only specific questions, blame you, or shame you (for your body or sex), to escape his guilt and pain. Being caught provides a totally different experience that aggravates and makes the information traumatic, but also the process of discovery.

I have had wives with proof of an affair, and it still takes him hours, or days, to get honest. Men will leave the house in silence for days, not talking to their wife who has been traumatized by what she now knows about him. How you receive the information about betrayal is a factor in your discovery day.

One or Multiple Disclosures

Partners experience disclosure in one of two ways. It can be a onetime event where all the general information about his acting out is disclosed (including when his behavior started and ended and what his behaviors were). I love when this happens because when we do a polygraph (weeks, months, and years later) the facts haven't changed. The wife can (at least) know he was honest at disclosure and he has been clean and honest since.

Then there is multi-disclosure, or as partners have described it, multiple stabbings, or dribbles of information. This is a man who keeps getting caught or is slowly forced to be honest because the wife "knows there is more." This can last for a week, months, years, or until they take a polygraph.

This makes discovery day unending. The wife is sentenced to tread water to stay in the marriage. Her soul cannot find a stable place because she doesn't know the truth.

To make matters worse, some counselors (not trained by me) will tell the wife to wait for months, or even years before he gives her full disclosure. Even when disclosure happens, he shares only what he wants to share, and a polygraph is not used to validate what is said. (There are some exceptions). If a therapist thinks they have this power, you may be in the wrong office. The sex addict, cheater, or intimacy anorexic heals a whole lot quicker if they tell the truth, rather than carry the shame with them daily. The wife and marriage can also have a better chance to heal with the truth, rather than putting disclosure off.

Remember not all therapists who say they treat sex addiction are sexually sober. It is legitimate to ask the therapist (male or female) when was the last time they masturbated, viewed porn, or had sex outside of marriage. If they can't, or won't answer this question, you may consider a different counselor. You can also ask if they are in recovery and have a polygraph to support their clean date. Mine hangs in my office.

I have seen so many women in unnecessary pain due to delayed disclosure. I personally take polygraphs and so does my clinical team because: 1) I want you to know there is a clean safe place for you and 2) I don't ask my clients to do something I am unwilling to do myself. I took my first polygraph when my pastor fell, and I was 19 years clean. Now I am over 33 years clean which is verified by a polygraph.

Sorry for the rant, I have just seen so many women pay emotionally and physically from delayed disclosure. How you receive disclosure is an important variable on your discovery day.

His Response to Heal

A variable I see with partners on discovery day is his response to heal. A man who discloses and then makes a plan to heal, provides a different experience than the man who says, "I don't have a problem," "I don't need help," "I'll just stop," or "If you have a problem with it, that's your problem."

A man who clearly wants to heal has tried (or is willing to try), various forms of accountability including counseling, talking to his spiritual leader, reading books, accountability software, or attending a local twelve step group. We have had men call to schedule an Intensive prior to disclosing to his wife, so he could show her he was really serious about making changes.

This is not the experience for some partners. I wish it was. Anger, shaming, blaming, not taking responsibility for his behavior (and worse), not caring or being indifferent, are all initial or ongoing responses to getting caught. Exposure of infidelity, sex addiction, or intimacy anorexia may expose what he truly loves, himself and his addiction. Remember men protect what they love and love what they protect.

The harsh reality for some women is exposing them to the fact that they are not loved, valued, or cherished by the men they love. This is true even though they have given their life, heart, sexuality, years, or decades serving them. I have sadly seen women take months (or years) trying to accept that she is less important than his acting out behavior. This is the woman who demands he read this book, watch this DVD, or go to this therapist. If his response to getting caught isn't a self-motivated desire to heal and is seen by lack of recovery behaviors, you are not accepting his lack of care for you and his choice to not heal.

In pointing out his disposition to heal as a variable, you see the possibility of women having two totally different experiences on discovery day. Regardless of his choice, however, you can choose to heal from this car wreck he chose for your life.

Your Trauma History

One unseen variable on discovery day is your trauma history. One woman may have grown up in a great family. Her mother was nurturing, and her dad told her she was amazing, smart, beautiful, and could do anything. She felt loved and secure even until marriage. She dated but had good boundaries and hit some bumps in the road, but no guy cheated on her, or shamed her body, or sexually. She did not experience the deaths of people close to her. For this woman discovery day is her first real trauma and her first real betrayal.

This type of partner has no reference point for his object reality choices to lie, view porn, or cheat. She is truly in shock. This is the first time pain has riveted through her body, soul, and spirit. This is the first time she has ever felt fractured. However, because this is her first trauma and she has been secure throughout her development, she can be more buoyant to fight through the trauma.

The other woman who has been abandoned by a mother or father, was sexually abused, raped, had an abortion, or multiple men cheated on her, comes to a discovery day differently. If she has not worked toward healing her past, then the current trauma can be experienced very differently than the woman without a trauma history.

This woman has several traumas and cracks from the past. She may have picked up an addiction to medicate these prior traumas. She may have gone to counseling in the past; however, the partner betrayal trauma is so intimate and multi-dimensional it can aggravate or reactivate the earlier trauma.

This woman may have created a negative or worthless narrative about herself from earlier traumas.The current trauma actually serves as a reinforcement of her past negative or worthless narrative. This women's negative narrative can complicate her recovery journey, regardless of his choices.

Others

A factor on discovery day (and the days ahead) has to do with "others." There are the images of "others" in porn. These "others" are often remote and not an immediate threat to the marriage.

There are the anonymous "others" where he acted out in one-night stands, with women at bars, or with women while traveling.

There are also the professional "others," such as prostitutes and massage parlor workers.

"Others" could be his coworkers or remote acquaintances of yours. There are sadly the "others" that are close girlfriends of yours, or even family members.

"Others" on discovery day are a huge factor. The "who" matters to you especially if it involves real people. All "others" including porn is real pain and real trauma. Each woman processes the "others" differently.

All betrayal is betrayal. All pain from betrayal is real and valid. The betrayal by porn is still betrayal. The betrayal from adultery, no matter with whom, is betrayal. The betrayal from being denied sex and intimacy with an intimacy anorexic husband is also betrayal and real pain.

"ALL PAIN FROM BETRAYAL IS REAL AND VALID."

Your "others" story is going to be unique to you both on discovery day and on your journey to heal. Every woman is allowed to process her pain as she addresses the "others" issue.

Resiliency Factors

In my 30+ years of working with partner betrayal trauma, I see variables that factor into how a woman navigates through the trauma of being betrayed by their partner. These factors are for your consideration as you take your unique journey to heal. A key factor in the Partner Movement is that I truly believe each partner should be seen as a person, a soul, not a label of co-addict or codependent. You are you and you are unique. Understanding some of these factors can help you see why your experience might be different than others.

In the sexual abuse field, there is acknowledgement that sexual trauma affects each person differently. One sexually abused person can become crippled emotionally for decades, and another becomes stronger and more successful despite the sexual abuse. In the field of classic literature, there is what is known as resiliency factors that include:

1. Family of Origin: This formative support (or lack of support) contributes to how a woman experiences relationships and establishes trust or mistrust of her world. These relationships also model how to address pain and the people that cause pain.

2. Trauma History: As we discussed earlier, this is a significant variable.

3. Spiritual Foundation: A woman with a clearly formed spirituality will go through trauma differently, with an added resource than a woman with an unclear, or vague spirituality. Also, women with a well-developed spirituality will often have women in her life that share her faith. These other women usually are the betrayed partner's initial, or ongoing support team.

4. Mental Illness: If a woman has no mental illness she will definitely navigate the partner betrayal trauma differently than a woman who has a psychological disorder. A woman who has a disorder, but is not diagnosed, is at a disadvantage on her partner journey. A woman with a true disorder can be stuck because of this lack of self-understanding.

The most common disorder I see in working with partners is depression. If depression is not assessed (and it could be caused by low thyroid or testosterone) then the energy to heal from the current trauma may be unavailable. If someone has histrionic personality disorder it can be the reason why she has difficulty regulating her emotions, even after a significant time of recovery has passed. Betrayed partners with borderline personality disorder are challenged by feeling rejected by their spouse's behavior. Partners with obsessive compulsive disorder can have difficulty regardless if the obsession is about themselves, or their spouse's behaviors.

To be fair, psychological disorders are also seen on the man's side. These include narcissism, antisocial personality disorder, depression, anxiety, ADHD and so on. It is also a challenge for him to heal if these are not diagnosed early in recovery.

Also, I have found when treating both spouses in the marriage, neither may have a full psychological disorder. The couple may be experiencing other features that can aggravate the couple in recovery, if not assessed. It is best practice, if a couple isn't making any progress after months of attempting recovery, to have both take a psychological test to clarify any unseen issues that may be hindering recovery.

Addictions

A woman with addictions of her own will have some challenges that a woman without addictions has in her partner journey. Addictions help us escape pain, past or present, but at the expense of our emotional development. These addictions include food, shopping, anger, as well as potential chemical addictions.

As you go through your partner journey (even early on), it is important to feel the rejection, pain, trauma, and shock throughout your recovery process. Journal, call other women, go to our Partner Facebook Group for partner support, pray, talk to a therapist, but feel the pain. Escaping through addiction will most likely exacerbate that addiction in your life.

Physical Health

Your body goes through the trauma with you. If a woman has been in a marriage with intimacy anorexia, her body has already been impacted. If sex addiction or infidelity is also part of her story, the body can be significantly impacted.

"TRAUMA IS A FULL "BEING" EXPERIENCE—SPIRIT, SOUL, AND BODY."

If you have been eating your way out of the pain from your marriage, this can also impact your health. Discovery day is a life changing day. I recommend women get serious about their nutrition, stretch and exercise regularly, experience healthy touch through massage, and get your thyroid and hormones checked.

Trauma is a full "being" experience—spirit, soul, and body. You want to take care of you. Abandoning your body during a traumatic experience (such as betrayal), can complicate your life down the road.

A woman who practices good self-care (prior and during the early phase of her recovery), does better. She eats well, sleeps, and exercises. Her physical stress is better managed which helps manage the emotional roller coaster she is on because of discovery day.

Sexual Health

A woman who initiates sex, is confident and creative sexually, has orgasms regularly, and can talk about sex at a mature level, is less likely to make his poor choices about anything to do with her sexuality.

A woman who is not sexually mature, can't talk about sex or during sex, doesn't initiate sex or is not creative sexuality, will have more challenges comparing herself to the porn, or the emotional or sexual affairs.

Her sexual history, sexual trauma, or rape can also be factors in her journey sexually through the partner betrayal. Let me be very clear (no matter how sexually mature you are or aren't), you did not in any way cause his choices.

He chose his behavior and you are not responsible for his choices at all.

Financial Health

A woman who has wealth, whether from her own work, business, or inheritance, or she knows she could acquire it through a divorce, approaches this journey differently than a woman without resources.

A woman who hasn't worked (for whatever reason,) with no real savings or retirement, has an additional challenge in this journey. If she sees herself without skills or abilities to make it on her own, she processes this journey differently than a woman with economic stability (independent of her husband.)

This is a factor to be honest about in your partner journey.

For some, this is a really important part of the decision process in recovery. If this is you, get support around this issue as you journey away from discovery day.

Him vs. Me

The factor of Him vs. Me is important on discovery day and moving forward in recovery. However, of all the factors we discussed, this one is the hardest for me to communicate, so I will do my best.

The woman who makes his bad choices 100% about him (his brokenness, immaturity, addiction, etc.), process discovery day and the rest of the days from a different vantage point, than women who make his poor choices somehow about them.

The woman who takes some, or most of the blame for his choices, does discovery day and the rest of the journey differently. She stays in the grief stage for a longer time focusing on issues such as: "If I was (or wasn't) bigger, smaller, sexier, liked sex more, praised him more, cleaned the house better, or dressed nicer and so on..."

This woman is looking at herself to blame for his bad choices. Sometimes she thinks if she can control this, or that variable about herself, then his bad behavior will stop. How me-centric or he-centric she is, is a factor in her partner betrayal trauma recovery.

Her Support

Discovery Day is a terrible day, in and of itself. However, this day faced alone can add to the pain. I have had countless women, through no fault of their own, become alone after getting this information. The heaving, crying, praying, traumatizing stillness, faced alone is really difficult.

Some partners, in an emotional reaction, reach out to their family, or even their children. Some reach out to a friend or spiritual mentor.

Having support on discovery day is best, but rarely can it be planned. I have had men wait until they came to their Intensive to expose their betrayal, because they wanted their wife to have a week of support.

After discovery day, support (and I would say the more intelligent support the better), is absolutely a huge variable in the partner recovery journey. Women who try to go it alone, don't reach out, don't go to group, or talk to a counselor, can triple, or more than triple the time to heal. Time alone does not remove a bullet if you have been shot. A bullet requires help, or you will limp for a very long time.

You all had a discovery day. However, your discovery day is unique to you. There are many factors that shape your discovery day, as well as your journey as a partner of betrayal trauma. You are "you." Your journey will be unique to you as I have described here. However, getting support and correct information can make your journey more successful as you heal.

"AFTER DISCOVERY DAY, SUPPORT, IS ABSOLUTELY A HUGE VARIABLE IN THE PARTNER RECOVERY JOURNEY."

3

Betrayed

As a partner of someone who has committed infidelity, has a sex or porn addiction, or has intimacy anorexia, you have been betrayed. Unlike a bullet that hits you in a certain location, or a car wreck that injures you in several places, this trauma hits all of you.

Partner betrayal trauma is unique among any and all forms of trauma. In sexual abuse, you did not choose the other person. The perpetrator of your sexual abuse didn't stand up before God, friends, and family, and promise he would forsake all others and love, honor, and cherish you.

Partner betrayal trauma is unique because it affects the understanding of your past, present, and future. This trauma affects the experiences of your entire timeline of your marriage or relationship—the vacations, sexual encounters, anniversaries, special holidays, children's birthdays—the entire timeline.

Partner betrayal trauma is also unique because it impacts all areas of your life. Your spiritual, emotional, sexual, financial, and physical life are all impacted.

Lastly, partner betrayal trauma is unique because it impacts all your relationships. You now have a secret. A secret you did not choose or create, but now you carry the burden of this secret. Every relationship is an opportunity to tell, or not tell. The dilemma of the secret alone is quite burdensome to the partner who has been betrayed.

In this chapter, I want to go through the variety of ways that you have been betrayed. I don't do this to rip scabs off of you. I do this to acknowledge and validate your betrayal. You have been betrayed and it is important to understand (early on in your recovery) how betrayal impacts multiple areas of your life.

In this chapter, we compare the results from *the Weiss Relationship Trust Questionnaire* where we asked women how much they trusted their husband (or significant other) **before** and **after** betrayal. The questionnaire is organized using a 5-point Likert scale with 1 = No Trust (*Not at All*) and 5 = High Trust (*Totally*).

Overall Trust

In Chapter 1, we talked about women being all in regarding their trust level of their husband or significant other. Overall trust is a strong indicator of how committed women are in their relationships with their husbands or significant others. Below you see the tremendous impact on overall trust of the women who participated in our research study.

Prior to your knowledge of betrayal, did you trust your husband/significant other?

1. 5% 2. 8% 3. 9% 4. 27% 5. 51%

After your knowledge of betrayal, do you trust your husband/significant other?

1. 60% 2. 21% 3. 12% 4. 6% 5. 1%

Comparisons of overall trust show how significant trust declines following betrayal. While 78% of women trusted their husband or significant other before betrayal, this number plummets to 7% after the knowledge of betrayal occurs.

Emotionally

Way before your wedding day you gave a sacred gift to this man. You might not know the exact moment, but you know that this gift was given and fully given. You gave him your heart.

That's right, you gave your husband that very deep part of yourself that connects to every emotion you'll ever have. At some moment, you looked in his eyes and said to yourself, "I am all in."

You shared your past accomplishments and scars with him. You shared your dreams and aspirations, not only of yourself, but of your children. You showed up when he needed support and encouragement. You overlooked flaws and showed love.

Your heart and emotions were all in and he chose to betray you. In that moment, whether it was months, years, or decades of his sex addiction, porn, or infidelity, his behavior said to you, "Your heart has little or no value to me. I am going to do what I want."

The moment you discovered his betrayal, you felt many things, but one of those things was feeling abandoned in your heart. Your heart was betrayed and your emotions and heart will need to be on a journey of healing, regardless of his future choices. Here are the results related to emotional trust before and after betrayal.

Prior to your knowledge of betrayal, did you trust your husband/significant emotionally:

1. 8%   2. 10%   3. 17%   4. 27%   5. 38%

This number statistically reinforces what I see in my office with women who are emotionally all in. A total of 65% of the women who participated in the study say they trusted their husband or significant other emotionally. As you can see, the hearts of these women were all in when they got hit with his betrayal.

Then we asked the same women how much they trusted their husband or significant other emotionally after betrayal, and here are the results.

After your knowledge of betrayal, do you trust your husband/significant other emotionally?

1. 63%   2. 19%   3. 11%   4.5%   5. 2%

The top two scores went from 65% to 7%. This is a total reversal of emotional trust.

You can clearly see how betrayal impacts you emotionally. Your feelings of emotional betrayal are real and valid. You will choose your path toward healing from your emotional betrayal, but it is real and valid for you to feel emotionally betrayed.

Spiritually

I have worked with thousands of partners of betrayal trauma. These women come from every spiritual perspective you can imagine. I have worked with women who are

Christians (of all types), Buddhists, Hindus, Native Americans, Muslims, Agnostics, and women with no spiritual background, or interest in spirituality.

Regardless of their spiritual background, all women have a spirit which is that inner part of you that connects to the bigger "God." The spirit is a real part of all of us. Often, it's your spirit that first perceives something is not right in your marriage or relationship.

Women with strong faith beliefs often have a husband (or significant other) who shares these strong spiritual beliefs. One such belief is, "Thou shalt not commit adultery." These couples believe God said this and meant it for their protection. It is also something that many couples mutually agreed upon in their relationships. I have worked with women who say the spiritual connection with their husband is the primary reason they married him. I have also worked with hundreds of pastors and the wives of spiritual leaders who have been spiritually betrayed by their husband or significant other.

Spiritual betrayal trauma is very real. From my experience, the more spiritual a woman is (regardless of the form of spirituality), the more she feels spiritually betrayed.

His betrayal can raise all kinds of spiritual questions for her. Sometimes she will blame God for "allowing" this to happen. She might question God's love for her in the wake of the betrayal from her husband or significant other.

Spiritual betrayal is a valid and significant part of the betrayed partner's experience. Here are the results related to spiritual trust before and after betrayal.

Prior to your knowledge of betrayal, did you trust your husband/significant other spiritually?

1. 12% 2. 15% 3. 16% 4. 25% 5. 32%

The majority of women (57%) trusted their husband/significant other spiritually. As you can see, you were building your dreams with God and your husband or significant other. Following betrayal, spiritual trust diminishes significantly.

After your knowledge of betrayal, do you trust your husband/significant other spiritually?

1. 54% 2. 23% 3. 9% 4. 11% 5. 3%

Only 14% of women trust their husband or significant other after betrayal (again a total reversal of these scores). Your spirituality, worldview, sense of safety, and purpose have all been impacted by the choice of your husband or significant other to betray you.

I will highlight here for a moment that it is your husband or significant other who betrayed you, not God. God cried as He watched him betray you. He saw every sad act he committed. He grieved at his choice to use his free will to cause pain.

Your husband or significant other is 100% responsible for the betrayal you have experienced and feel. Spiritual betrayal is valid and usually this journey requires help from some "sisters" from a similar spiritual community as yours. I encourage you to walk with God (as you understand Him to be). He is a great source of comfort and wisdom for you as you heal.

> "YOUR HUSBAND OR SIGNIFICANT OTHER IS 100% RESPONSIBLE FOR THE BETRAYAL YOU HAVE EXPERIENCED AND FEEL."

Socially

The impact of betrayal socially is both external and internal. From an internal perspective many partners of betrayal trauma often have lingering feelings of "Do they know?" or "Did they know?" This applies to his friends, family, co-workers, neighbors, and even acquaintances. This feeling of who knew can be heightened if the affairs were long term, people you personally knew, co-workers, women from a social or spiritual community, or if you live in a small town.

The external social betrayal makes you feel like hiding. You don't want to go grocery shopping, or to the mall because you might run into her, them, or someone who knew about it. There is a wide range of emotions, thoughts, and experiences when you meet someone who knows. In your mind you are trying to assess what they're thinking: "Do they think I didn't give him enough sex?" "Am I bad in bed?" and so on. These questions are symptoms of the social betrayal from the choices of your husband or significant other.

Even women who have not experienced infidelity, or sex addiction can have social awkwardness if they are married to an intimacy anorexic. These women are unwanted, in an emotionless and often sexless marriage. They walk around with this secret daily. They often have to pretend in public because their private life is so painful. They also feel betrayed because of their husband's choice not to love them.

There is also the aspect about not being able to relax socially when you're with your husband or significant other. "Is he checking her out?" "Does he want her?" "Is he lusting after that person?" Again, your entire social experience is impacted because of his choices.

We asked women in our research to respond to their trust level socially before and after the knowledge of his betrayal. Here are the responses.

Prior to your knowledge of betrayal, did you trust your husband/significant other in social situations?

1. 7%   2. 12%   3. 20%   4. 23%   5. 38%

Prior to betrayal, 61% of women trusted their husband for significant other in social situations.

After your knowledge of betrayal, do you trust your husband/significant other in social situations?

1. 42%   2. 29%   3. 16%   4. 10%   5. 3%

In social situations, a total of 61% of women trusted their husband or significant other before the knowledge of betrayal. This number dropped significantly (to 13%) after the knowledge of betrayal.

Again, you can see statistically (not just from your own experience), that part of your betrayal experience affects you socially.

Sexually

Sex can be the most intimate experience between two people. This is not just a symbol of giving all of yourself to the other person. The giving of yourself to another person (along with the vulnerability it brings), continues for years or multiple decades.

Women have all levels of sexual confidence or insecurity. This is by far the deepest level of betrayal. Regardless of your faith or lack of it, sex is perceived by most women as sacred. This perception of sex heightens when you marry and your husband promises to close all doors to all others, for the rest of your lives.

The response to betrayal especially with others or pornography is varied. Some women go into a hypersexual state, wanting more sex, getting more creative sexually, and being more engaged verbally during sex. Some women go blank inside, they are numb and have no desire (or are even disgusted thinking about sex), with him. In this area of betrayal, there is no "normal" or even predictability.

The internal conflict of being a sexual being and desiring to be sexual, while being betrayed through your one source of sexuality (your husband or significant other), is mind blowing.

This aspect of betrayal is very deep in your being. Your journey will be unique to you based on sexual variables that include: your disposition, sexual history, beliefs about sex, marriage, hormones, age, sexual confidence, level of obsession in general, and the meaning you give his sexual behavior.

Counselors can be helpful, or hurtful here. You're going to have to listen to your heart and you may need polygraphs from him to feel safe again. I highly recommend two videos that have nothing to do with sex itself but are helpful on moving through this trauma. The two resources are *I Need to Feel Safe* and *Unstuck*. The concepts in these DVDs can help you navigate many of the feelings you might have around these two questions, "This doesn't make sense to me," and "How could he do this?"

On the subject of sexual betrayal and healing from sexual betrayal, I could write an entire book because the complexities of who you are, who he is, the relationship history, and many other variables that come into play when moving from sexual betrayal toward sexual health.

I will say, I have personally helped thousands of women go from sexual betrayal to the best sex with their husband ever. There is hope, but this is a unique journey for you.

In our research we asked women to rate their level of sexual trust before and after knowledge of disclosure. Here are the results.

Prior to your knowledge of betrayal, did you trust your husband/significant other sexually?

1. 6% 2. 14% 3. 11% 4. 26% 5. 43%

Prior to betrayal, 69% of women trusted their husband or significant other sexually.

After your knowledge of betrayal, do you trust your husband/significant other sexually?

1. 61% 2. 20% 3. 10% 4. 8% 5. 1%

Sexual trust dropped significantly following betrayal (from 69% to 9%).

Numbers don't lie. Sexual trust following partner betrayal is devastating for women. This betrayal is so painful and a difficult journey to restore. If you choose to restore sexual trust and want help, I recommend going to www.aasat.org and click on "Find a Therapist." Here you will find trained counselors who understand this journey. Or you can call my office to speak to a female counselor who has years or decades of experience in this area.

The last thing you need is "canned" or "extreme" advice from a counselor who is not certified to treat you, or the sex addict. If you go online, 90% of counselors who say they treat sex addicts (or their spouses), have zero training or certifications in this area. You want someone who truly understands you and the issues you are working through (whether it is his infidelity, sex addiction, or intimacy anorexia). Ask your therapist about their sexual health and initiation in their own relationships. You want to make sure they are living a sexually healthy life if they are guiding you toward sexual health.

Financially

Your financial betrayal is also unique to you. Your husband or significant other may have spent almost no money on his acting out, with himself or others. He may have spent thousands, or hundreds of thousands on his acting out behaviors.

Your husband or significant other might be highly successful, both in making and managing money. He might be lousy, at both making or managing money. In my experience, those who are betrayed financially are devastatingly betrayed. He may have cashed in the children's college fund, or he might have secret accounts. Your husband or significant other may have given "her" money for a car, purse, or house. He may have bought "her" expensive gifts, trips, and so on.

The pain of knowing how he took money from you, or your children, (money that could have been used in positive ways), and gave it to himself, "her," or used it for illicit behavior, is a betrayal all by itself.

His choice to betray you financially is very real. This aspect of betrayal can also include losing his job, career, retirement, license, or partnerships as a result of his behavior. The mindlessness and recklessness of his choices could impact you financially for years, or even decades.

The economic impact on you and your family from his betrayal speak for themselves. Below are the results of financial trust before and after betrayal.

Prior to your knowledge of betrayal, did you trust your husband/significant other financially?

1. 10% 2. 12% 3. 14% 4. 27% 5. 37%

Financial trust before betrayal was 64%.

After your knowledge of betrayal, do you trust your husband/significant other financially?

1. 38% 2. 17% 3. 17% 4. 19% 5. 9%

Financial trust following knowledge of betrayal dropped from 65% to 28%. This decrease in financial trust is a significant one in the marriage relationship.

In my experience, there are only a small percentage of couples who are impacted financially for quite a long time. I have seen men who control their own income (i.e. business owners, entrepreneurs, sales people, etc.) who significantly increase their net worth (even in one year), if they actually do their recovery and heal.

I have also seen women (who have been economically dependent their entire life on their husband or significant other), catapult themselves into economic independence. Your journey will be yours and you might have to become your own financial hero.

Parenting

The needs of your children are totally dependent on their ages. Children of preschool and early school years are quite different from high school or college- aged children. This family situation is also quite different than when your children are grown with families of their own.

Your husband could be anywhere on the continuum of being a good parent, or not. His level of support and engagement could also be anywhere on that continuum regardless of his betrayal of you.

Here you will have to render how much of his behavior impacts day-to-day parenting, or overall parenting. I will say if a man fails in parenting, this compounds your experience of betrayal.

If he is absent emotionally, spiritually, or physically (on a consistent basis), due to his infidelity, sex addiction, or intimacy anorexia, you will experience trauma in the area of parenting due to his choices.

Responses from women in our research regarding their trust level of their partner as it relates to parenting are as follows.

Prior to your knowledge of betrayal, did you trust your husband's/significant other's parenting?

1. 5% 2..19% 3. 31% 4. 23% 5. 22%

A total of 45% of women trusted their husband or significant other with parenting before betrayal.

After your knowledge of betrayal, do you trust your husband's/significant other's parenting?

1. 27% 2. 20% 3. 26% 4. 20% 5. 7%

After betrayal scores for trust with parenting decreased from 45% to 27%.

If parenting is impacted in your situation, this betrayal will have added grief and ongoing consequences in your family's life. You will want to spend some time truly grieving this area of loss from his betrayal.

General Responsibilities

Prior to your knowledge of betrayal, did you trust your husband/significant other with general responsibilities?

1. 5% 2. 14% 3. 23% 4. 31% 5. 27%

Over half of women (58%) trusted their husband or significant other with general responsibilities before knowledge of betrayal.

After your knowledge of betrayal, do you trust your husband/significant other with general responsibilities?

1. 20% 2. 25% 3. 22% 4. 26% 5. 7%

Following the knowledge of betrayal, only 33% of women said they trusted their husband or significant other with general responsibilities.

Extended Family

Extended family includes your parents, siblings, aunts, uncles, and their families as well as his parents, siblings, aunts, uncles, and their families. The extended family can know some, or all of the truth of his behaviors of betrayal. Or your families may know nothing about his choices to betray you. This could still have an impact on you because you now carry the secret, and you may feel different around them.

This aspect of the betrayal trauma is also unique to your

situation. The decision to tell (or not to tell), was probably already made by one, or both of you.

Your family history as a couple is also unique. Your husband or significant other might be a wanted or unwanted member of your family (or vice versa), for you with his family. There are levels of family rules, pride, traditions, expectations, competition, religion, or economic issues that all play a part in how you navigate extended family issues.

Here if you need help, reach out. Families are at every place on the spectrum, from not being able to forgive him (even years after you have), to forgiving him early on in the process. They may have limited knowledge but all families have opinions on infidelity, sex addiction, or intimacy anorexia.

Your family will love you the best that they can. However, the more hurt they are by his betrayal (for you and the rest of the family), the more difficult it can be to restore these relationships.

From our research we had women respond to how they trusted their husband/significant other in regard to extended family. Here are their responses.

Prior to your knowledge of betrayal, did you trust your husband/significant other in other extended family relationships?

1. 6%   2. 16%   3. 21%   4. 24%   5. 33%

The total score of trusting in extended family relationships was 57%.

After your knowledge of betrayal, do you trust your husband/significant other in other extended family relationships?

1. 24% 2. 24% 3. 25% 4. 15% 5. 12%

The score of trust in extended family relationships after betrayal dropped to 27%. There is a significant shift in trust in extended family relationships after betrayal is known.

Extended family relationships can be challenging after betrayal. I would seek wise counsel prior to informing or engaging extended family in your process. This, of course, is unique to your situation. Once the decision to inform your family occurs emotionally, or with deliberation, the impact on them cannot be determined or changed.

Keeping Their Word

Prior to your knowledge of betrayal, did you trust your husband/significant other to keep their word?

1. 9% 2. 12% 3. 21% 4. 29% 5. 29%

The total score of trusting your husband or significant other to keep their word before knowledge of betrayal was 58%.

After your knowledge of betrayal, do you trust your husband/significant other to keep their word?

1. 45% 2. 28% 3. 11% 4. 13% 5. 3%

After knowledge of betrayal, trusting your husband or significant other to keep their word drops significantly from 58% to only 16%.

Trust

Follow Through with Commitments

Prior to your knowledge of betrayal, did you trust your husband/significant other to follow through with their commitments?

1. 10%   2. 14%   3. 19%   4. 29%   5. 29%

Similar to trusting your husband or significant other to keep their word, 58% of women said they trusted their husband or significant other to follow through with their commitments prior to knowledge of betrayal.

After knowledge of betrayal, do you trust your husband/significant other to follow through with their commitments?

1. 42%   2. 28%   3. 12%   4. 14%   5. 5%

Again, on the trust scale of trusting your husband or significant to follow through with their commitments this number drops significantly from 58% (before betrayal) to 19% (after knowledge of betrayal).

<u>It's Real</u>

I wrote this chapter with one primary motivation. I want you to feel validated that your partner betrayal trauma is real, and it is multifaceted. The pain, grief, and tears you have from his betrayal is real, and I deeply honor that pain. Your journey through partner betrayal will take courage, strength, and support, regardless of his choices. You are an amazingly strong woman and you can make this journey. I encourage you to stay supported and loved by women (like you) who are forced to take a journey they didn't choose.

"YOUR JOURNEY THROUGH PARTNER BETRAYAL WILL TAKE COURAGE, STRENGTH, AND SUPPORT, REGARDLESS OF HIS CHOICES."

4

Your Body

I have told women, thousands of times, that betrayal trauma affects your spirit, soul, and body. In this section, I will reveal what our partner betrayal research helped us understand about the impact betrayal has on you physically.

You are organically complex as a human being. You are not just a body, mind, soul, or spirit—you are all of these—all of the time. When trauma occurs, it will impact each organically complex human very differently. Your physiological response to betrayal is unique to you.

Trauma of any type is not a formula, if X happens then every woman has a Y response at the same level.

As you read the results of this research study some of this will resonate with you greatly, while others will not apply because you are 'you." You respond in specific ways to the trauma only you experienced. However, collectively we see the overall impact that occurs in women who have experienced partner betrayal trauma.

Somatoform

In our research we used the Patient Health Questionnaire (PHQ), a self-report measure developed to identify five common health conditions (Spitzer, Williams, & Kroenke). These health conditions include:

Somatoform Disorder
Major and Other Depressive Syndromes
Panic and Anxiety Syndromes
Eating Disorders
Alcohol Abuse

Partners of betrayal trauma were evaluated for all five health conditions before and after knowledge of betrayal.

Somatoform Disorder

Below is a complete listing of symptoms covered for Somatoform Disorder. The questions are scored on three-point Likert scale of (not bothered at all, bothered a little, or bothered a lot). A patient is provisionally diagnosed with Somatoform Disorder if they report they are "bothered a lot" by three or more of the symptoms. Below is a complete list of symptoms for this health condition. Results from the "bothered a lot" category are shown to illustrate the impact on the physical symptoms of women before and after betrayal occurred.

Bothered A lot

	Before	After Trauma
Stomach Pain	18%	58%
Back Pain	16%	35%
Arm, Leg, Joint Pain	15%	37%
Menstrual Pain	21%	24%
Pain During Intercourse	16%	25%

Headaches	24%	55%
Chest pain	8%	31%
Dizziness	4%	26%
Fainting	0%	6%
Racing Heart	17%	62%
Shortness of Breath	5%	39%
Constipation	18%	46%
Nausea	15%	53%

Prior to awareness of betrayal, 76% of women reported low symptom severity and only 24% of women would qualify for a diagnosis of Somatoform Disorder. Out of the 13 symptoms, only two (headaches and menstrual pain) were the most common symptoms.

However, after the awareness and impact of his betrayal the scores changed significantly. After knowledge of betrayal, a total of 71% of women in the study reported symptoms severe enough to warrant a diagnosis of Somatoform Disorder. The most common symptoms reported were stomach pain, chest pain, racing heart, and nausea. You don't have to be a psychologist to figure this out. Betrayal has a huge impact on the physical body of the partner experiencing betrayal.

"BETRAYAL HAS A HUGE IMPACT ON THE PHYSICAL BODY OF THE PARTNER EXPERIENCING BETRAYAL."

Your body most likely will be impacted by partner betrayal trauma. As you can see from this research, all 13 symptoms moved up some or a lot after betrayal was discovered. The increase in the symptoms of Somatoform Disorder is seen regardless if the betrayal came through addiction, infidelity, or intimacy anorexia.

Depression

Depression can be present due to physical issues like brain chemistry. Depression symptoms also parallel low thyroid or low testosterone symptoms. Depression is also reflected in the grief process, since partners of betrayal trauma experience incredible loss.

In the first printing of *Partners: Healing from His Addiction* (2001) which started the Partner Movement, we surveyed 39 women about depression *prior* and *during* their relationship with a sex addict. In that study, we found a 43% increase in depression for women who were in a relationship with a sex addict. The most common symptoms these women experienced were low energy or fatigue, depressed mood, feelings of hopelessness, unable to sleep or oversleeping, poor appetite or overeating, and feelings of restlessness or being slowed down.

As a clinician for partners, I can validate that many women have increased depression after disclosure. Again, your experience will be unique to you. However, this is an area where most partners of betrayal trauma are impacted and should be looked at as part of your overall partner recovery plan.

In our current research study, depression was also measured. Below are the results of a major depression diagnosis before and after awareness of the betrayal of a spouse or significant other.

Before betrayal 26% met criteria for a depression diagnosis
After betrayal 88% met criteria for a depression diagnosis

This is a 62% increase in major depression symptoms for partners of betrayal. This research concludes most partners of betrayal trauma are different as a result of the trauma caused by the husband or significant other in their life. You are not crazy, most women act and feel different after being betrayed.

Below are the results of depression symptoms of women who reported having these symptoms "nearly every day," before and after betrayal trauma.

Depression Symptoms
"Nearly Every Day"

	Before	After
Little interest or pleasure in doing things	1%	7%
Feeling down, depressed, or hopeless	16%	81%
Trouble falling or staying asleep, or sleeping too much	22%	81%
Feeling tired or having little energy	22%	81%
Poor appetite or overeating	19%	74%
Feeling bad about yourself	21%	65%
Trouble concentrating	12%	73%
Moving slowly or fidgeting more than normal	5%	37%
Thoughts of self-harm	5%	33%

Similar to Somatoform Disorder every symptom of major depression went up significantly in our research. This validates that your body has been impacted by the betrayal you have experienced. I want to say to you again, you are not crazy, and the impact of betrayal trauma is real.

If you are experiencing depression, I recommend women:

1. Get thyroid or adrenals checked

2. Get hormones (including testosterone) checked

See a doctor that specializes in depression, not just a general practitioner

Panic/Anxiety Symptoms

This part of the scale measures for panic syndrome as well as other anxiety syndrome. Here are the results from the partners we surveyed.

Before Knowledge of Betrayal

Met criteria for Panic Syndrome	9%
Met criteria for Other Anxiety Syndrome	17%

After Knowledge of Betrayal

Met criteria for Panic Syndrome	19%
Met criteria for Other Anxiety Syndrome	71%

Again, those who experience partner betrayal trauma are impacted significantly with increased anxiety. More than 50% of the participants reported the following symptoms "more than half of the days."

1. Feeling nervous
2. Feeling restless
3. Feeling tired
4. Having muscle aches
5. Having trouble sleeping
6. Having trouble concentrating
7. Becoming easily annoyed

These symptoms will be unique to you in intensity, frequency, and duration. If this is part of your healing, seek a psychiatrist or medical doctor, as well as a counselor to heal from the impact of betrayal trauma.

Binge Eating & Bulimia

Overall, binge-eating and bulimia did not bother the participants in this study either before or after betrayal. While the results were less significant, this is still an important area to address.

Before betrayal

Met criteria for Bulimia 7%
Met criteria for Binge Eating Symptoms 5%

After betrayal

Met criteria for Bulimia 12%
Met criteria for Binge Eating Symptoms 7%

There are only slight changes in both binge-eating symptoms and bulimia for the participants of our current study.

In the self-report data from our earlier study (2001) there were also slight increases in eating disorders such as anorexia nervosa and bulimia. However, most of the women reported that they struggled with overeating (84%) and turning to food (59%) to cope during their relationship with a sex addict.

Eating disorders, or issues with food, may or may not be a problem for you as a result of partner betrayal trauma. If you struggle with these issues on your journey toward recovery, be honest about it and get the support you need so you can heal.

Alcohol

Alcohol is something that people who are suffering consume to cope from a variety of trauma, or changes in their lives. Alcohol was also assessed in our research. Below are the before and after results of alcohol use for partners of betrayal trauma.

Alcohol Abuse Before 10%
Alcohol Abuse After 16%

Although there is an increase in alcohol abuse for women experiencing partner betrayal trauma, the increase is small, indicating that most women were not impacted by alcohol abuse. However, in my experience, those who turn to alcohol tend to do so in a significant manner.

In this chapter we discovered and validated that partner betrayal trauma specifically has an impact on your body. The impact is real. I would strongly recommend you go through the *Partner Betrayal Trauma Workbook* to identify your specific areas of impact on your physical body. In the workbook you can start an action plan for the unique journey of healing from the areas you identify.

I have witnessed many women heal in their partner journey. Addressing the impact of trauma is a significant aspect of your journey. It is important that you take this part of your recovery seriously so you can heal, and lessen the long-term consequences from betrayal trauma.

The bravest and strongest women I have ever met are partners who heal. Evaluating your body's impact is your responsibility. You did not cause the trauma. However, you are responsible to assess and heal from the trauma. I hope this helps you discover the hero in you.

"THE BRAVEST AND STRONGEST WOMEN
I HAVE EVER MET ARE PARTNERS WHO HEAL."

5

Esteem

In previous chapters, we discussed how partner betrayal trauma impacts your body, your trust, and other aspects of your personal life. In this chapter, we will discuss how betrayal affects your self-esteem and sexual self-esteem.

For this part of the research study, we used Rosenberg's Self-Esteem Scale to assess overall self-esteem. Below are the results before and after knowledge of betrayal by women in the study.

	Before	After
High Self-Esteem	56%	29%
Medium Self-Esteem	34%	44%
Low Self-Esteem	10%	27%

This comparison to me is helpful. Looking at the research about 50% of women with high self-esteem are hugely impacted. In my clinical experience, this is what I see from women who start in the high self-esteem category. This woman feels safe in her relationship, successful in her career, has a good body image, and then literally gets shot, or shot multiple times (dribbled disclosure), and her self-esteem drops significantly. Again, this is a normal response, but not all women experience this.

I have also seen a number of women who get shot by betrayal who maintain high self-esteem. These women are usually financially independent and successful, or just stable inside. From the beginning, these women knew that this was 100% about him and his poor choices, and it really doesn't affect her self-esteem. Again, every woman's journey is unique.

The results also show an increase in women with a medium level of self-esteem, mostly because of women who drop from the high self-esteem category. Low self-esteem scores also increase.

To further the "unique" journey narrative shared throughout this book, the self-esteem area is particularly interesting. A total of 45% of women in the study maintained their pre-betrayal level of self-esteem. Their self-esteem did not move at all because of the betrayal from their husband or significant other, whether it was infidelity, sex addiction, or intimacy anorexia.

Of the women surveyed, 11% reported an increase in self-esteem following the knowledge of betrayal. You might ask, "Why?" While the response to this question is unique to each woman, what I have heard women tell me for decades is, "It's a relief to know I am not crazy!" Knowing the truth and knowing they were right, helps some partners turn the full responsibility of the choices over to their husband or significant other.

In 2001, when we asked women to report on their self-esteem the results were similar.

There was a 20% decrease in the High Self-Esteem category and a 20% increase in Medium (or Average) Self-Esteem.

For this study, the Low Self-Esteem category was divided into two areas: Low Self-Esteem increased by 11% and Very Low Self-Esteem increased by 29%.

When you compare these two studies of partners eighteen years apart, you see a similar trend. Self-esteem drops significantly for women who have been betrayed. On the intake we developed in the *PRT (Partners Recovery Training)*, one of the first questions we ask partners to assess the impact of his betrayal, is about their self-esteem.

General Thoughts

In this section, I want to address self-esteem in general terms from what I see in my office on a day-in, day-out basis.

During 5-Day Intensives, I cover the hurting of a partner in great detail. One of the first questions I ask a partner is about her self-esteem. I also ask partners about their feelings of "worthiness."

The feeling of worthlessness is common among partners. In most cases, feelings of worthlessness proceeded her marriage. Often the husband capitalizes on his wife's feelings of worthlessness, by reinforcing these feelings by his words, behaviors, or lack of behavior toward her.

"Worthless" is tricky because often this voice speaks to you and befriends you early on in your life. You begin to internally believe you have less value than others around you. I have had many women tell me they hear an internal voice that says

- You're not enough.
- You'll never be enough.
- You're fat.
- You're lazy.
- You quit everything.

- You're a fake.
- You're ugly.
- Nobody wants you.
- You failed.
- You make really bad choices.
- Nobody loves you.
- You're stupid.

Women who hear this voice usually hear it often and loudly, and in many cases, this voice is unspoken, an ongoing feeling, or becomes an obsession. Some women overfunction to compensate for the fear that others might find out about them. Other women underfunction to keep validating that she is worthless.

This worthless voice can come from many experiences. Let me list some of the primary experiences women that hear the voice of worthlessness have in common:

- Abandonment by one, or both parents
- Emotional or physical abuse
- Emotional or physical neglect
- Sexual abuse
- Rape
- Abortion
- A silent, disconnected father
- A critical mother
- Being mother's scapegoat or slave
- Lack of affirmation from parents
- Lack of success
- Poor romantic relationships
- Abandoning self to an addiction

You may, or may not, have to take the journey of healing or building self-esteem. However, I know this journey is real for many partners.

I wrote a book that never was supposed to be published, a book called *Letters to My Daughter.* When my daughter Hadassah went to college, I handwrote and mailed a letter to her everyday during her first year of college. In the letters I wrote to my daughter, I focused on how to live life from a dad to his only daughter. I didn't know she was sharing these letters with her friends in the dorm, until one day someone who stayed at our house started quoting some of these ideas to me. It was then that I realized the impact of a dad's voice to a young woman.

I have had 50- and 60-year-old women reading this book in the lobby who were crying because their own father failed to affirm them. The absence of a father's voice was a foundation for their feelings of worthlessness.

"THE ABSENCE OF A FATHER'S VOICE WAS A FOUNDATION FOR THEIR FEELINGS OF WORTHLESSNESS."

If your journey of healing includes addressing issues of worthlessness, we have a DVD and workbook called "*Worthy.*" This series has helped many women heal from feelings of worthlessness, to experience their worth independent of the past or present choices of their husband.

Whatever the impact of your betrayal trauma, I believe in you to heal so you can be among some of the most awesome women I have ever met—partners of betrayal trauma.

Sexual-Esteem

One question I wanted to get more solid data on is the issue of sexual-esteem. Partner betrayal trauma is unique in the entire family of trauma, mainly because the person who betrays you and causes the trauma is your husband or significant other.

"PARTNER BETRAYAL TRAUMA IS UNIQUE IN THE ENTIRE FAMILY OF TRAUMA."

In marriage and in long-term sexual relationships you are all in, which includes your sexuality. Also, the type of betrayal you experienced involves sexuality. He either cheated with another person, cheated by regularly being sexual with himself, watched porn, went to strip clubs, or he cheated on you sexually by withholding love, sexuality, or romance by staying married to himself through intimacy anorexia. All these traumas are sexual and intimate in nature.

In our current study of partners of betrayal trauma, we utilized the *Sexuality Scale* (Snell & Papini). This scale measures the following three aspects of human sexuality:

1. Sexual-Esteem (a positive view and confidence in the ability to experience one's sexuality in satisfying and enjoyable ways)

2. Sexual-Preoccupation (the tendency to focus on sex to an excessive degree)

3. Sexual-Depression (experience of feelings of depression regarding a person's sex life)

All items on the scale are answered using a 5-point Likert scale and scores range from -20 (negative responses) to +20 (positive responses). Here are the results from the partner betrayal trauma research study.

	Before	After
Sexual-Esteem	1	-5
Sexual-Preoccupation	-8	-7
Sexual-Depression	0	3

Before the betrayal was known, women in the study had a slightly positive sexual self-esteem (with an average sexual self-esteem of 1). Women were not preoccupied with sex (with an average score of -8). Before betrayal was known, women were relatively neutral about their sex lives (average score of 0).

Scores on all of the scales changed after knowledge of betrayal. Scores on sexual-esteem decreased from 1 to -5 which is a significant drop in sexual-esteem for women after betrayal is known. Scores on sexual-preoccupation increased slightly from -8 to -7, showing essentially the women were still not preoccupied with sex. Finally, scores on the sexual-depression scale increased from 0 to 3. Although the overall depression is not severe, it does represent an increase in sexual depression overall. After betrayal, women feel less "good" about their sexuality and sexual experience. When a partner of betrayal trauma says she feels different sexually after betrayal, she clearly does.

There are many variables that impact sexual-esteem for women. Let me cite a few.

- Her sexual education
- The sexual beliefs/behavior of her family of origin
- Her cultural/religious sexual beliefs
- Her sexual confidence
- Her sexual experiences
- Rapes, or attempted rape
- Sexual abuse
- Husband's sexual maturity and love towards her

- Her confidence with her body
- Her confidence with intimacy
- Her general personality

Your sexuality is unique to you. You may have great sexual-esteem and still feel that way after disclosure of betrayal. Some women do. You might have had high sexual-esteem and it totally tanked after disclosure. You might have had low sexual self-esteem which improved after disclosure.

Your sexuality is a gift. Your sexuality is yours to express, create and heal, protect and honor. I have seen thousands of women find their sexuality, their sexual voices, create boundaries in healthy ways, and have the best sex of their lives after recovery.

I have also seen women recoil from sexuality (some only for a short season), and some never heal sexually. The impact of betrayal on your sexuality is yours alone. Your journey of recovery is yours alone to walk towards a healthy sexuality for you.

"YOUR SEXUALITY IS YOURS TO EXPRESS, CREATE AND HEAL, PROTECT AND HONOR."

6

Intimacy Anorexia

Many women have experiences with a spouse who has intimacy anorexia, or they themselves have it (perhaps as a reactive form of intimacy anorexia from the betrayal trauma).

In the mid-90s, Patrick Carnes and I, along with seven other key national treatment providers convened in a room in Dallas, Texas. We discussed a phenomenon we were all witnessing in our male sex addiction clients. These men were not having sex with their wives (even after being in sex addiction recovery). Patrick went on to write a book called *Sexual Anorexia: Overcoming Sexual Self-Hatred* (1997) which focused mostly on withholding sex from your spouse. However, this didn't really capture what I was seeing in my office. So that same year (1997) I made a video called *Sexual Anorexia* which highlights what I observed: male sex addicts (who were clearly anorexic), didn't mind having disconnected sex with their wives.

Later, I coined the term "intimacy anorexia" which captures the experiences of women and men around the globe. In this chapter, I will briefly explain what many of you may be experiencing in your marriage, how intimacy anorexia is defined, and the characteristics associated with it. After this brief discussion, I will share with you what over 100 women reported in our partner betrayal trauma research study. I find the results very interesting.

Intimacy Anorexia: *Intimacy anorexia is the active withholding of emotional, spiritual, and sexual intimacy from one's spouse.*

The following section is an excerpt from the book *Intimacy Anorexia: Healing the Hidden Addiction in Your Marriage.*

Intimacy anorexia can impact other primary relationships like children and extended family. However, it is my experience that it is mostly manifested in the marital relationship.

I want to parse this definition just a little bit. I find this is helpful for partners of betrayal trauma to go a little deeper before moving into the characteristics.

The word "active" is by far the word in the definition of intimacy anorexia most disputed by the anorexics themselves. Everyone around the intimacy anorexic agrees that the word "active" is very appropriate for what they are observing and experiencing. Although it's clear the behaviors of withholding and pushing their spouse away have been repeated hundreds (or even thousands of times), the intimacy anorexic wants to claim no intention for these behaviors.

"THE WORD 'ACTIVE' IS BY FAR THE WORD IN THE DEFINITION OF INTIMACY ANOREXIA MOST DISPUTED BY THE ANOREXICS THEMSELVES."

Active means there is a choice. Often there is a clear intention on the part of the anorexic to create pain for the spouse as a by-product of making the anorexic safe, distant, or in control. Active means each act of withholding intimacy from their spouse, is an act for which the anorexic is responsible, and can change with recovery.

"Withholding" is quite simple to understand. I have something, but I won't give it to you. An intimacy anorexic has intimacy, but he gives it to friends and colleagues and simply withholds it from his spouse.

Emotional intimacy says to the spouse, "Here is my heart, flaws and all. I open it as much as I can and behold your heart as well."

"

"EMOTIONAL INTIMACY SAYS TO THE SPOUSE, HERE IS MY HEART, FLAWS AND ALL."

Everyone in the real world of relationships knows that pain is part of the relationship process. Emotional intimacy does not say, "I connect, give myself and receive you, if you promise never to hurt me, see or mention my flaws, or disagree with me." This conditional intimacy and irrational need for safety in intimacy anorexics is very common. Withholding emotional intimacy says that regardless of how much of my heart I can access and give to you, I will not share my emotional or authentic self with you. This is a choice.

The spiritual part of a human being is by far the most intimate part. Our spirit is not only the universal place that connects us with God, but our spirit is a place of knowing, discerning, and having intuition (a sense of things that goes beyond facts).

Spirituality with our spouse is one of the most sacred things on earth. Regardless of the manifestation of worship, prayer, meditation, or other connecting rituals, when we share this inner person with our spouses, we share our authentic self (more purely than mere words can express).

The intimacy anorexic says, "No! I'm not letting you into that sacred place." The religious intimacy anorexic will pray with others, but will rarely pray, worship, or open their spirit up to their spouse. Not allowing the spouse in spiritually is intentional. Again, regardless of skill or background, we all have a spirit. Giving the spiritual part of ourselves to our spouse is an important ingredient for intimacy in marriage.

Sexual intimacy can be electrifyingly intimate inside a marriage when both spouses are giving and receiving within the sexual encounter. Just as we are emotional and spiritual, we are all sexual. We were sexual from the first slap on the behind at birth and will be sexual until our last breath.

Sexuality is far more than an act—it is part of who we are. Intimacy anorexics can either deny they are sexual or engage as little of themselves as possible in the act of sexuality. The majority of anorexics, male and female, do not mind the act of sex. It is the giving of their heart or connecting during sex that is scary. The anorexic would say that he will give you his body, but not his soul, or spirit during sex.

This one-dimensional sex (physical sex), over time, can become unsatisfying for the spouse, or even an unattractive proposition altogether. Some anorexics purposely reinforce sex in a negative way so their spouses will not want to be sexual with them.

A smaller number of intimacy anorexics want nothing to do with sex. They avoid sex by shutting themselves down and over time, starve or punish their spouses with the lack of sex (intentionally creating a sexless marriage at the cost of their spouse's happiness). This desire to be unknown is intentional. It says, "I will not let you in, no matter what pain I intentionally inflict on you. Too bad for you."

Withholding or sabotaging sex is a part of the intimacy anorexia pattern for some and a primary part for others. However, it is a very small part of the intimacy anorexia pattern for some.

Intimacy is the ability for me to let you behold me, flaws and all. I am flawed and loved, and you are flawed and loved. I let you see me, and you let me see you. I have heard some say intimacy is *in-to-me-see*. That's clever, and I think you get the point. The intimacy anorexic prefers to be regarded as altogether good. Prior to recovery, the intimacy anorexic has great difficulty letting their spouse see their flawed self. For most intimacy anorexics, the only answer to an invitation to intimacy is "No."

"INTIMACY IS THE ABILITY FOR ME TO LET YOU BEHOLD ME, FLAWS AND ALL."

Intimacy can be scary for anyone, regardless of gender. For the intimacy anorexic, intimacy can be terrifying beyond belief. Interestingly enough, intimacy is the only solution for an intimacy anorexic.

As mentioned earlier, there is something about marriage that demands what the anorexic wants to withhold, and that is long-term emotional, spiritual, and sexual intimacy. Even a marriage between healthy people can be challenging at times.

The anorexic applies a variety of strategies to create and maintain distance in the relationship. This distance allows the intimacy anorexic to feel safe, protected, and in control. The intimacy anorexic is not going to allow himself to be threatened by genuine intimacy. The strategies anorexics use effectively to create distance differ from couple to couple. However, over time, you can see anorexic strategies build a fortress against their spouse.

Characteristics

Busy - The first characteristic of an intimacy anorexic is being so busy you have little time for your spouse. This is a very common characteristic for most intimacy anorexics. This does not necessarily mean the spouse travels all the time, though that could definitely be a way to avoid intimacy. Busyness can include anything from productive activities, volunteering, reading, computer time, or anything else that justifies why the intimacy anorexic cannot be with his spouse in a quality manner.

"Busy" takes on so many forms, it could be a book all by itself. Any of these behaviors could be fine in a marriage if the anorexic stayed connected to his spouse. In the absence of connecting, "busy" becomes a way for the intimacy anorexic to actually withhold intimacy—even the potential for intimacy—through avoidance.

Blame - Blame, as an anorexic characteristic, is almost universal. When an issue or problem comes up in the marriage, the anorexic blames or puts responsibility on the spouse for it, before seeing their contribution to the problem or issue. As you understand intimacy anorexia better, how intimacy anorexics wants to be in the "good box" all the time, it makes being flawed, irresponsible, thoughtless, careless, and bad less desirable to discuss (if you are the anorexic).

Blaming is almost reflexive for many anorexics. I am absolutely amazed at how much the emotional survival of the anorexic is at stake if they are found to be flawed like the rest of us. Often, they cannot be honest about their intentional withholding. Starving their spouse directly affects the behavior they receive back from their spouse.

Withholding Love - The anorexic often has a difficult time perceiving the intangible nature of withholding love. To withhold love is not to love your spouse the way you know to, or how they have asked to be loved. Each one of us wants to be loved, and yet we all experience being loved in many different ways. Spouses may want emotional sharing, long walks, or a thoughtful note, or gift that says, "I was thinking of you." Some just want help around the house, or with the children. However, the spouse needs to be shown love, and the anorexic already knows how the spouse wants to be loved.

"TO WITHHOLD LOVE IS NOT TO LOVE YOUR SPOUSE THE WAY YOU KNOW TO, OR HOW THEY HAVE ASKED TO BE LOVED."

Here is how to know what type of love your spouse needs, and if you are withholding it from them. The anorexic convinces his future spouse that they love them in the way they receive love. This leads him to the decision to marry. Think back to when you dated your spouse. First, what meant a lot to him or her? Second, when you really get in trouble in your marriage (or the marriage is threatened) what do you do to make up, or show you care? Finally, if your life was dependent upon your answer, could you say you know how your spouse feels your love the most? If you are the intimacy anorexic, and you agree now that you know how your spouse receives love, then why are they doing without it? If you do not have a clear, rational reason without blaming, then let me suggest you are actively, intentionally withholding love from your spouse.

Withholding Praise - The withholding of praise is also a significantly recurring behavior for intimacy anorexics. To withhold praise is to not share with your spouse their positive qualities and their positive impact on your life. Let's go back to, "as if your life was dependent upon your answer." If you had to write ten things that are amazing and positive about your spouse, or how they impact your life in a positive way, my bet is, again, you could absolutely make a list pretty quickly.

If you are an anorexic, think about the last week, or month, and how frequently you intentionally praised your spouse. How often are you praising your spouse in front of their family, your friends, or even your children? If you are the spouse of an anorexic, reflect on this as well. When was the last time you really received heartfelt praise without asking for it from your spouse?

"HOW OFTEN ARE YOU PRAISING YOUR SPOUSE IN FRONT OF THEIR FAMILY, YOUR FRIENDS, OR EVEN YOUR CHILDREN?"

All of us have amazing positive qualities. Anorexia, over time, closes this positive vision and tends to create focus on the flaws of the spouse.

If you have not been praising your spouse regularly for who they are and all they do, may I suggest that you could be actively and intentionally withholding praise from them?

Withholding Sex - By far, of all the behaviors that are characteristics of intimacy anorexics, withholding sex is probably the easiest to measure. It is also the most obvious.

Withholding sex from your spouse is avoiding having sex, sabotaging sexual encounters, or not connecting emotionally during sex. You can tell whether you are the spouse, or the anorexic by analyzing the last time you had sex. It might not be as easy for the anorexic to remember the last time they sabotaged a sexual encounter, or whether it was before, during, or after the encounter. It is even harder for the anorexic to remember withholding emotionally and spiritually during sex, or really giving all of themselves. Any of these behaviors can be a way of withholding sex.

Here are some examples from the *Intimacy Anorexia Workbook*:

During sex, do you look at your spouse or close your eyes?
Do you think of other things to do during sex?
Do you fantasize about others or porn during sex?
Do you communicate positively during sex?
Are you silent during sex?
Do you act as if you dread sex?
Do you hurry your spouse to get it over with?
Do you leave your spouse emotionally or physically after sex?
Do you shut your spouse down when talking about sex?

Withholding Spiritually - This spouse might not notice the withholding of spirituality. Some of my clients have been spiritual leaders, pastors, rabbis, and even medicine men who did not connect with their spouses spiritually. Withholding spiritually is withholding spiritual connectedness from your spouse. This means, regardless of faith practices or the lack thereof, there exists no real spiritually connective behavior with the spouse. The anorexic might be religious to the hilt, but not spiritually authentic in the presence of his spouse.

I have heard countless excuses, especially from the religious anorexic (regardless of faith) that include: I do this just by myself. It's not my personality. My spouse is too spiritual (or not spiritual enough), so I do not connect with her spiritually. Regardless of the rationalization, there is an absence of spiritual connection between the intimacy anorexic and their spouse.

Feelings - This characteristic can be described as being unwilling or unable to share feelings with one's spouse. Having difficulty sharing feelings is also a universal characteristic of the intimacy anorexic. As stated earlier, addictions hinder emotional development.

If you are the spouse of an intimacy anorexic, you may have difficulty remembering a time when your husband voluntarily shared feelings with you without having to write the "emotional check" for the experience. If the anorexic's image of the marriage is threatened, or they really blows it somehow, you can expect them to share some feelings. However, that positive behavior fades away within a week or two after the activating event.

Sharing one's feelings is an act of authenticity that can be scary and difficult for an intimacy anorexic. Their unwillingness or inability to share feelings can be intentional, so as not to give you love the way they know you like it.

Criticism - Ongoing or ungrounded criticism which leads to distance in the marriage, is the seventh characteristic of intimacy anorexia. This criticism consists of low-grade put downs toward the spouse, noticing what they do wrong, or just regularly pointing out that their ideas are bad.

The ungrounded criticism has little to do with reality. This strategy might be to push the spouse away or to throw them off the trail of something. Either way, it intentionally creates distance.

Anger/Silence - Not all intimacy anorexics use silence or anger. However, those that use anger or silence use it with a vengeance. This intimacy anorexia characteristic can be described as *any use of anger or silence to push away, punish, or control the spouse.*

Money - The characteristic of controlling or shaming the spouse about money issues is probably the least common among intimacy anorexics. However, those who employ it do so with an iron fist. Most of the anorexics who control or shame with money, do so by keeping the spouse ignorant of the finances, giving the spouse an allowance, making the spouse ask for money, and refusing to allow the spouse to have a credit card or checkbook.

There is the other side of controlling through money as well. I call it controlling through abundance. This spouse has substantial money, but controls with it. The spouse's attitude is as follows: I buy you everything, so do not complain about a lack of intimacy, love, or sex. This type of control through money is not as obvious as control through not giving.

Shaming the spouse about money can also be a part of this intimacy anorexic characteristic. In this case, it is perfectly okay for the intimacy anorexic to spend money on anything they desire, but their spouse has to account for everything, or is criticized for purchases, even legitimate ones.

Roommate - The characteristic I have seen in a vast majority of intimacy anorexics' marriage relationships can be summed up with the keyword "roommate." *The spouse of the anorexic feels like, or has stated feeling like, a roommate.* I have heard this same comment so many times from spouses that I often add it to the end of my assessment of clients for anorexia.

Intimacy Anorexia Test

Below is the *Intimacy Anorexia (IA) Test* (a free test found at www.intimacyanorexia.com). Someone would answer this about themselves or about their spouse. However, because intimacy anorexics have challenges acknowledging their flaws, this test is more accurate if they answer as they think their spouse might answer it, or they have their spouse answer it for them.

Do they stay so busy that they have little time for you?

Yes No

When issues come up, is their first reflex or response to blame you?

Yes No

Do they withhold love from you?

Yes No

Do they withhold praise from you?

Yes No

Do they withhold sex from you or are they not emotionally present during sex?

Yes No

Do they withhold spiritual connection from you?

Yes No

Are they unwilling or unable to share their authentic feelings with you?

Yes No

Do they use anger or silence to control you?

Yes No

Do they have ongoing or ungrounded criticism (spoken or unspoken) towards you?

Yes No

Do they control or shame you regarding money or spending?

Yes No

Do you feel more like a roommate than a lover in your relationship?

Yes No

You can take the test the way your spouse might answer about you. Then take the test how you would answer about your spouse.

Once you take the test then add up all the "yes" responses. If you or your spouse have more than five "yes" responses, then you are having issues with intimacy anorexia. If you have ongoing conversations about feeling like you are roommates, or like brother and sister instead of lovers or spouses, you could be married to an intimacy anorexic.

There is help if someone wants help. The spouse of an intimacy anorexic suffers greatly. We have books and workbooks called *Married and Alone*, as well as counseling or Intensives for this issue. A woman who has been married (for any length of time) to an intimacy anorexic has experienced partner betrayal trauma, just as much as those married to a sex addict or someone who has committed infidelity.

Research

The summary of the research shows that before betrayal, 20% of those surveyed identified themselves as IA. After betrayal 60% of women identified themselves as IA. This huge increase in intimacy anorexia symptoms means that the pain of trauma creates a pattern for safety (out of fear, uncertainty, and grief), that looks a lot like intimacy anorexia. This form of IA (reactive intimacy anorexia) can be short-term but really is women reacting to the trauma of betrayal.

This gets tricky as a therapist because some women are clearly IA prior to his betrayal, due to their family of origin, sexual trauma, poor relationship with her father, or her own sexual addiction. If there is a legitimate question here, I have women watch the DVD *Reactive Intimacy Anorexia* that's part of the Intimacy Anorexia Training at www.aasat.org. After watching this DVD, most women are able to distinguish if they are IA or Reactive IA for their therapist.

There was a fascinating find in this research of intimacy anorexia as it related to husbands. The women scored their husbands both before and after on the *Intimacy Anorexia (IA) Test.*

Before betrayal (whether infidelity, sex addiction, or intimacy anorexia was reported), 89% of women said their husbands had intimacy anorexia! This is an extremely high number, but we definitely see a lot of male intimacy anorexics in our center.

Here is where it gets interesting. In the research, after the betrayal was known this number decreased to 68% of women reporting their husbands had intimacy anorexia. That 22% drop is significant. This finding may be due to the fact that after betrayal, the behavior of the husband showed up differently—be it more affectionate, or just less distance and disconnectedness. However, if the intimacy anorexic is not treated, this may only be temporary and could reoccur.

There is healing for both the intimacy anorexic, or the married and alone spouse regardless of gender. If this is part of your story, make sure it becomes part of your recovery story as well.

"THERE IS HEALING FOR BOTH THE INTIMACY ANOREXIC, OR THE MARRIED AND ALONE SPOUSE REGARDLESS OF GENDER."

7

Post Traumatic Stress Disorder (PTSD)

This is going to be a very important piece of understanding your experience as a partner of betrayal trauma. Post-Traumatic Stress Disorder also known as PTSD has become a part of the conversation for partners mostly because of the work of Dr. Barbara Steffens and Marsha Means, and their book, *Your Sexually Addicted Spouse: How Partners Can Cope and Heal* (2009).

Let's review some of the history of the Partner Movement again. First, you were called co-addicts. Then in 2001, my book *Partners: Healing from His Addiction* started the Partner Movement based more on research than the co-addict model. Many years later, the PTSD conversation evolved in the Partner Movement (for which I am grateful). Currently, a group of people have used a child sexual abuse model and applied it to betrayed partners, basically stating that the relationship of the perpetrator is a factor in the equation of trauma for a partner who has experienced betrayal.

This leads us now to the partner betrayal trauma conversation that helps us better understand the experience of partners who have been betrayed.

Here again is the partner model quoted from the *Partners Recovery Training* from the American Association for Sex Addiction Therapy (AASAT).

1. Every partner is absolutely unique and worthy of honor for whom they presently are.

2. The partner has no responsibility for the addict's addiction or acting out.

3. Partners come anywhere on the continuum of spiritual, emotional, physical, financial, sexual, and social health.

4. Any partner who takes responsibility for herself can heal and grow in areas she deems necessary.

5. The addiction often creates collateral damage that is best to heal from as early as possible.

6. There are no core beliefs or attributes for partners. They are all unique beings.

Now let's talk about clinical PTSD which I will define in general terms. Then I will share results from the research study that validate that betrayed partners do experience PTSD symptomology. Then I will translate this term for women who specifically experience partner betrayal trauma. Having a mutual language is important for the partner community as well as the clinical community. I long for the day when partners can go to a counselor without being labeled or misunderstood.

General PTSD

Here let's talk frankly about what counselors call PTSD from the Diagnostic & Statistical Manual of Mental Disorders. According to DSM-5, PTSD occurs when:

You were exposed to one or more event(s) that involved death or threatened death, actual or threatened serious injury, or threatened sexual violation. In addition, these events were experienced in one or more of the following ways:

1. You experienced the event

2. You witnessed the event as it occurred to someone else

3. You learned about an event where a close relative or friend experienced an actual or threatened violent or accidental death

You experienced repeated exposure to distressing details of an event, such as a police officer repeatedly hearing details about child sexual abuse

Here is largely where there is a disconnect for a partner seeking help for her partner betrayal. She shares with her counselor that she is experiencing PTSD. The counselor asks, "Who died, had their life threatened, or thought they were going to be raped?" The partner says, "No one." And the clinician says, "You're not having PTSD, you're overreacting honey."

I am on your side, and I have research to prove you are experiencing PTSD symptoms as a partner of betrayal trauma (not as someone who experienced a near-death experience). This disconnect and language barrier has hurt many partners when the real pain and symptoms they are experiencing are not validated.

According to the DSM-5, there are eight criteria for the diagnosis of PTSD:

Criterion A

You were exposed to one or more event(s) that involved death or threatened death, actual or threatened serious injury, or threatened sexual violation. In addition, these events were experienced in one or more of the following ways:

1. You experienced the event

2. You witnessed the event as it occurred to someone else

3. You learned about an event where a close relative or friend experienced an actual or threatened violent or accidental death

4. You experienced repeated exposure to distressing details of an event, such as a police officer repeatedly hearing details about child sexual abuse

Criterion B

You experience at least one of the following intrusive symptoms associated with the traumatic event:

1. Unexpected or expected reoccurring, involuntary, and intrusive upsetting memories of the traumatic event

2. Repeated upsetting dreams where the content of the dreams is related to the traumatic event

3. The experience of some type of dissociation (for example, flashbacks) where you feel as though the traumatic event is happening again

4. Strong and persistent distress upon exposure to cues that are either inside or outside of your body that are connected to your traumatic event

5. Strong bodily reactions (for example, increased heart rate) upon exposure to a reminder of the traumatic event

Criterion C

Frequent avoidance of reminders associated with the traumatic event, as demonstrated by one of the following:

1. Avoidance of thoughts, feelings, or physical sensations that bring up memories of the traumatic event
2. Avoidance of people, places, conversations, activities, objects, or situations that bring up memories of the traumatic event

Criterion D

At least two of the following negative changes in thoughts and mood that occurred or worsened following the experience of the traumatic event:

1. The inability to remember an important aspect of the traumatic event
2. Persistent and elevated negative evaluations about yourself, others, or the world (for example, "I am unlovable," or "The world is an evil place")
3. Elevated self-blame or blame of others about the cause or consequence of a traumatic event
4. A negative emotional state (for example, shame, anger, or fear) that is pervasive
5. Loss of interest in activities that you used to enjoy
6. Feeling detached from others
7. The inability to experience positive emotions (for example, happiness, love, joy)

Criterion E

At least two of the following changes in arousal that started or worsened following the experience of a traumatic event:

1. Irritability or aggressive behavior
2. Impulsive or self-destructive behavior
3. Feeling constantly "on guard" or like danger is lurking around every corner (or hypervigilance)
4. Heightened startle response
5. Difficulty concentrating
6. Problems sleeping

Criterion F

The above symptoms last for more than one month.

Criterion G

The symptoms bring about considerable distress and/or interfere greatly with a number of different areas of your life.

Criterion H

The symptoms are not due to a medical condition or some form of substance use.

DSM-5 PTSD Diagnosis

In order to be diagnosed with PTSD according to the DSM-5, you need to meet the following:

- Criterion A
- One symptom (or more) from Criterion B
- One symptom (or more) from Criterion C
- Three symptoms (or more) from Criterion D
- Three symptoms (or more) from Criterion E
- Criteria F through H

I can hear many of you saying, "That's me!" and I hear you. However, most of the clinical community will not because

Criterion A (exposure to actual or threatened death, serious injury, or sexual violence) has not been met.

Let's unpack this definition of PTSD through the partner betrayal trauma model. It's true, you didn't see a person murdered and you weren't threatened to be killed.

However, through his betrayal (be it infidelity, sex addiction, or intimacy anorexia) marriage is threatened to be murdered, to sustain serious injury, or to be starved to death. Marriage is a real "being" in my thinking when I go back to Genesis, which most world religions call the creation story.

God created Adam as the first being and He took a while to make him a man (read my book *Miracle of Marriage* for more details). Many months, or years later, God made Eve. After God spent some time with Eve, He created His final masterpiece in the garden. This masterpiece is marriage (a three-being unit of Himself, man, and woman) where God said man and woman *become one.* Marriage is its own divine miracle creation, a sacred trinity. Marriage, like a baby, is not just a sperm (dad), or an egg (mom) but something way more, a completely different creation.

"

"MARRIAGE IS ITS OWN DIVINE MIRACLE CREATION, A SACRED TRINITY."

Your marriage is a created being. You were all in when you felt the bullets of his infidelity or sex addiction hit your marriage. You saw and experienced a near-death or murder of a marriage. You felt the similar pain of watching a murder when the attempted murder was perpetrated by the one person who vowed before God, family, and friends to protect this "being" called marriage.

If you experienced the ongoing intentional starvation of a marriage through his IA, you were exposed to a passive attempt at murdering your marriage through aggressive starvation. This is like watching a marriage in a concentration camp.

As partners, you totally get what I am saying. Your marriage is you, you are your marriage, and he put an emotional, sexual, financial, social gun to your head, or intentionally starved you. This is what near-death experience you were exposed to.

Sadly, I have witnessed this too, when I see a man murder a marriage in my office by choosing the other person, his addiction, or to stay married solely to himself (IA). The marriage literally dies right in front of me.

Partner Betrayal Trauma

Women who experience partner betrayal trauma share similar symptomology as PTSD. However, it is much clearer language to say "I am experiencing Partner Betrayal Trauma" than I am experiencing PTSD. This can also help the clinician to learn of your past experience.

Let's review the research findings we found. For this part of the study, I adapted the criteria questions for general PTSD, but applied them specifically to partner betrayal trauma. Here are the responses from women who participated in the study.

PTSD Criterion A - I felt that my marriage/relationship with him was severely threatened or could end, and experienced intense fear, hopelessness, or horror.

Yes	82%
No	18%

When I found out about his behaviors, I felt that my marriage/relationship with him was severely threatened or could end.

Yes	94%
No	6%

My response to finding out about his behavior included:

Intense fear	82%
Intense helplessness	86%
Horror	78%
None of the above	4%

PTSD Criterion B -Intrusive distressing memories, distressing dreams, flashbacks, psychological distress from trauma reminders, or physiological reactions to trauma reminders longer than a month.

Yes	83%
No	17%

Since finding out about his behavior, I have had intrusive distressing thoughts about his behavior.

Yes	97%
No	3%

If you have had intrusive distressing thoughts about his behavior it lasted:

Does not apply to me	4%
Days	3%
Weeks	0%
A month	1%
Several months	17%
A year	6%
Longer than a year	69%

Since finding out about his behavior I have had intrusive distressing dreams about his behavior.

Yes	74%
No	26%

If you have had intrusive distressing dreams about his behavior it lasted:

Does not apply to me	23%
Days	7%
Weeks	3%
A month	1%
Several months	24%
A year	5%
Longer than a year	37%

I have experienced reliving the experience of finding out about his behavior or what the behaviors were (i.e. flashbacks, illusions, hallucinations) like you were actually there again.

Yes	73%
No	27%

If you have had reliving experiences about his behavior it lasted:

Does not apply to me	25%
Days	7%
Weeks	1%
A month	1%
Several months	19%
A year	4%
Longer than a year	43%

I have experienced intense psychological distress when I have externally or internally been exposed to something that symbolizes or resembles his behavior.

Yes	87%
No	13%

If you have experienced intense psychological distress when you have externally or internally been exposed to something that symbolizes or resembles his behavior it lasted:

Does not apply to me	12%
Day	14%
Weeks	5%
A month	<1%
Several months	14%
A year	7%
Longer than a year	48%

PTSD criterion C - engages in persistent behaviors to avoid memories or reminders of the trauma lasting longer than a month.

Yes	91%
No	9%

I have exerted effort to avoid thoughts, feelings, or conversations about his behavior after disclosure.

Yes	72%
No	28%

The efforts to avoid thoughts, feelings, or conversations about his behavior after disclosure lasted:

Does not apply to me	25%
Days	6%

Weeks	5%
A month	0%
Several months	14%
A year	5%
Longer than a year	45%

I have exerted effort to avoid activities, places, or people that arouse recollections of his behavior.

Yes	89%
No	11%

The effort to avoid activities, places, or people that arouse recollections of his behavior lasted?

Does not apply to me	9%
Days	2%
Weeks	2%
A month	0%
Several months	15%
A year	6%
Longer than a year	66%

PTSD criterion D - negative alterations in cognition and mood lasting longer than a month.

Yes	92%
No	8%

I have an inability to recall aspects of information about his behavior after discovery.

Yes	30%
No	70%

I have experienced significant diminished interest/participation in important activities after finding out about his behavior.

Yes	88%
No	12%

After finding out about his betrayal, I have experienced feelings of detachment or estrangement from other people.

Yes	90%
No	10%

Since finding out about his betrayal, I have felt emotionally restricted.

Yes	85%
No	15%

Since finding out about his betrayal, I have a sense my future has been shortened.

Yes	77%
No	23%

PTSD criterion E - marked alterations in arousal and reactivity lasting longer than a month.

Yes	95%
No	5%

Check all the behaviors you have experienced since finding out about his behavior (from the list of five possible choices).

Difficulty falling asleep	87%
Irritability or outbursts of anger	80%
Difficulty concentrating	88%
Hypervigilance	75%
Exaggerated startled response	59%

PTSD Criterion F – The above symptoms last for more than one month.

The reporting of these questions relating to duration were included in the sections above for criteria B and C where the majority of women reported symptoms greater than one month.

PTSD criterion G – The above symptoms cause significant distress.

As a result of finding out about his behavior, I have experienced significant distress or impairment in social, occupational, or other important areas of functioning in my life?

Yes	92%
No	8%

Many of the women in this study suffered significantly from PTSD symptomology. Of the entire sample, 66% met the criteria for PTSD diagnosis. Interestingly, 90% of the women who participated in the study said they found out about the betrayal over 12 months ago. While the original event (of betrayal becoming known) occurred a while ago, over 66% of the women still had symptoms of PTSD one year later. Looking at the criteria for PTSD the women in this study reported:

They felt their relationship was severely threatened and they experienced intense fear, helplessness, or horror (Criterion A) 82%

Intrusive distressing memories, dreams, or flashbacks or psychological or physiological distress from trauma reminders (Criterion B) 83%

Engaging in avoidance behaviors because of the trauma (Criterion C) 91%

Negative thoughts or mood (Criterion D) 92%

Problems with irritability, hypervigilance, or sleep disturbances (Criterion D) 95%

Above symptoms have caused significant distress or impairment in functioning (Criterion E) 92%

The results of this study reveal quite a bit to you and hopefully to clinicians who want to help partners of betrayal trauma. These percentages suggest that PTSD symptomology is very prevalent in women suffering from betrayal, and this sort of betrayal is traumatic.

"THESE PERCENTAGES SUGGEST THAT PTSD SYMPTOMOLOGY IS VERY PREVALENT IN WOMEN SUFFERING FROM BETRAYAL, AND THIS SORT OF BETRAYAL IS TRAUMATIC."

Remember your experience is unique to you for so many reasons. This research validates the majority of experiences of partners of betrayal trauma. However, not all women experience PTSD symptoms, or they may not experience PTSD symptoms in the same way as you, or as intensely as you.

Your partner betrayal trauma recovery journey will be unique to you. Understanding the trauma can be a huge piece for you in your overall recovery journey.

"YOUR PARTNER BETRAYAL TRAUMA RECOVERY JOURNEY WILL BE UNIQUE TO YOU."

8

Betrayal Trauma

A recent development in the Partner Movement is the expansion of the definition of betrayal trauma to include women who have experienced betrayal trauma through infidelity, sexual addiction, or intimacy anorexia from their spouse or significant other. There is no one person to attribute this particular voice to in our movement.

These voices have read the works of Dr. Jennifer Freyd, *Betrayal Trauma: The Logic of Forgetting Childhood Abuse* (1996) and the book *Blind to Betrayal: Why We Fool Ourselves We Aren't Being Fooled* (Freyd & Birrell, 2013).

These are great books that mostly focus on childhood sexual abuse and adult sexual trauma. I think Freyd's work is best captured in the following quote from *Betrayal Trauma: The Logic of Forgetting Childhood Abuse*:

"Betrayal is the violation of implicit or explicit trust. The chosen and more necessary the relationship, the greater degree of betrayal. Extensive betrayal is traumatic. Much of what is traumatic to human beings involves some degree of trust (p. 9).

The contributions of Freyd to the field of trauma (especially sexual trauma), is significant. First, the premise of the relationship of the perpetrator of the victim is a factor to how the person experiences and processes the relationship.

Second, how dependent a person is may explain why a person may "forget" or incorporate the trauma to be able to function in life.

Freyd continues to develop and broaden the term trauma (outside of childhood sexual trauma), to include adult sexual trauma and other areas of trauma. In 2006, Goldberg and Freyd developed *The Brief Betrayal Trauma Survey (BBTS).*

I am committed to have the Partner Movement become more and more based on facts, rather than feelings, misinformation, experiences, or nothing at all. I want new voices to be heard but then truly validated. I believe the findings from the previous chapter on PTSD and the connection to betrayal trauma, give value and a "voice" to partners of betrayal trauma.

"I AM COMMITTED TO HAVE THE PARTNER MOVEMENT BECOME MORE AND MORE BASED ON FACTS, RATHER THAN FEELINGS..."

In the current research study, 141 women completed the *Brief Betrayal Trauma Survey (BBTS).* Let me, as quickly as possible, explain the structure of this survey to you. The objective of this survey is to assess the level of betrayal in a variety of potential traumas that a person could experience.

The survey consists of 12 questions which ask how many times a participant has experienced a trauma, and at what age.

Never
1-2 Times (Under 18)
1-2 Times (18 or Older)
1-2 Times (Both Under and Over 18)
More Than Twice (Under 18)
More Than Twice (Over 18)
More Than Twice (Both Under and Over 18)

The survey includes low betrayal items, medium betrayal items, and high betrayal items as defined by the authors. The high betrayal traumas are of the most interest in this research. Three of the 12 traumas are labeled high betrayal by Goldberg and Freyd (2006).

High Trauma
- Deliberately attacked by someone known
- Sexual assault by someone known
- Psychological abuse by someone known

Medium Trauma
- Witnessed known trauma
- Witnessed known attack
- Deliberately attacked by unknown
- Sexual assault by unknown
- Death of a child
- Other trauma

Low Trauma
- Natural disaster
- Accident
- Witness unknown trauma

Please don't email me, "Dr. Weiss, rape by an unknown person or death of a child is a medium trauma?" I know *all trauma is trauma* and each is unique which is why I resist categorizing trauma. However, this is not my test, so don't get stuck here. The real goal was frequency (how often trauma occurred) and at what age.

Also, note that infidelity, sex addiction (or any addiction), and intimacy anorexia were not specifically named as trauma in this survey. However, as stated throughout this book, because of the close relationship between a partner and their husband (or significant other), along with the degree of trust in this relationship, betrayal trauma from sex addiction, infidelity, and intimacy anorexia aligns with the category of psychological abuse by someone known (considered high trauma in this survey).

Here are results of the BBTS from the women who participated in our study.

Only 8% of women reported experiencing none of the traumas examined in the survey. The average number of traumas experienced was four, and the greatest percentage (49%) reported experiencing either two, three, or four of the traumas examined. None of the participants reported experiencing all 12 of the traumas, but two participants reported experiencing 11 of the 12 traumas.

The most common trauma reported from this group of women was psychological abuse by someone known (81%). However, 25% of women reported multiple instances before the age of 18 and 31% reported the trauma occurred both under and over 18. More research will need to be conducted to investigate this further. The least common trauma reported was the death of a child; only 10% of the same sample reported this trauma.

A total of 34% of women reported experiencing a deliberate attack by someone known, and 39% of the sample reported sexual assault by someone known. Only 15% of women reported not experiencing any of the high betrayal traumas, and another 17% of women reported experiencing all three high betrayal traumas at some point in their lives.

Discussion

I want you to reinforce that the BBTS was not, in any way, trying or attempting to measure PBT (partner betrayal trauma). This clearly was not their objective, as it has been ours for decades. While this is important work, it is not specifically related to what you are experiencing.

Also, if you look at three types of trauma from the high trauma category, they are similar to the PTSD model of being attacked or raped. This gives the partner of betrayal trauma a similar clinical disadvantage.

I want you to be aware of the studies, language, and criteria of the clinical community so you understand how partner betrayal trauma can be misunderstood. If a clinician uses the focus of betrayal trauma as defined by Goldberg and Freyd, without creating an application to your partner betrayal trauma, you can be at quite a disadvantage. They could ask whether you were attacked, raped, or psychologically abused by your husband or spouse. Some women have not experienced any of these traumas as defined here, and again, may feel dismissed or misunderstood.

"SOME WOMEN HAVE NOT EXPERIENCED ANY OF THESE TRAUMAS AS DEFINED HERE, AND AGAIN, MAY FEEL DISMISSED OR MISUNDERSTOOD."

The focus of the original betrayal trauma was not trauma related to infidelity, sex addiction or intimacy anorexia. I believe these are great people doing great work, just not specific enough to address most of what our focus and research has to offer specifically for you who suffer from partner betrayal trauma (PBT). This model of betrayal trauma is incomplete, and the language associated with it is difficult, making it hard to generalize to other types of trauma such as partner betrayal trauma. It is clear that more work needs to be done in this area.

Your trauma is unique and different from general trauma in many ways. I want to list just a few.

1. Your marriage is the most intricate of all relationships.

2. Your marriage is also the most interdependent complex relationship you can experience with another person.

3. The level of public/verbal trust that was promised to you gave you hope that this would not happen.

4. Your level of trust and vulnerability created the trauma to be multifaceted with multiple levels of fractures.

5. This particular trauma can affect many, if not all, your relationships.

6. This betrayal can impact you sexually, like no other relationship.

7. This betrayal can kill your marriage or significant other relationship.

8. This betrayal can change your financial and social future.

9. This relationship betrayal can impact your children and all your extended family relationships.

10. This betrayal can impact your very identity, personally and socially.

Every journey of healing will be as unique, as is each trauma. However, I really believe betrayal trauma is not exact enough language for partners to be clearly understood and validated by the clinical community.

I believe you have measurably, and clearly, experienced partner betrayal trauma. Partner betrayal trauma gives those who experience this unique trauma, and those who want to treat it, the same language.

"EVERY JOURNEY OF HEALING WILL BE AS UNIQUE, AS IS EACH TRAUMA."

9

Trauma Reset

We have talked a lot about trauma as we have traveled through these pages together. However, we have yet to talk about the opportunity trauma offers to those who experience it.

Remember every type of trauma is different, whether it be physical trauma, spiritual trauma, sexual trauma, legal trauma, or financial trauma. Also, every person who experiences trauma is different in a variety of ways that include age, race, health history, family of origin, spirituality, self-beliefs, and history.

Partner betrayal is unique as well. When a husband or significant other betrays you through infidelity, sex addiction, or intimacy anorexia, this is real trauma. What they did, how you found out, who you are, the stage of your life, self-belief, sexual history, trauma history, hormones, health and economic issues, all make your partner betrayal experience unique because you are unique.

However, as unique and wonderful each of the women I have counseled with are, there is a common dynamic of reset all women have to face.

Before I explain the reset opportunity, we have to do some traveling down an almost seventy-year old road together. When we are done traveling this road, I will talk about the inevitable reset opportunity you will face as a partner of betrayal trauma.

Human Development

In the 1950s, Dr. Erik Erikson created a very well accepted psychological development model of human beings. He presented developmental stages of life and the crisis at each stage of development. If we are successful in a positive way through the various stages, we continue in a positive direction. If we are unsuccessful in a particular stage, we move our development in a less fulfilling direction. Early on, parents play a significant role in our lives which will shape (for a season) how we experience our life.

Let's take a look at these developmental stages. Where I am going after you understand this can change your process as a partner of betrayal significantly.

Stage 1 Infancy to 18 months: Trust vs. Mistrust

You can't talk (with words), you can't move much, you can't meet any of your basic needs. You must trust others to meet every basic (and not so basic) need you have. Before you could utter a word, you made specific assumptions about your mother and father ,as well as general assumptions as to whether the world, or the people in it are safe, available, present, connecting, and if you can trust them. Or, you made nonverbal assumptions you can't trust these people, they are undependable, not present, or connected to you. You may not want to "come out and play" in this world because your experience tells you it's not safe. Hence you could specifically not trust your parents, or you could generalize that everyone in the world is not safe to you.

Stage 2 Toddler/Early Childhood: 18 months to 3 years: Autonomy vs. Shame

Here we begin to differentiate ourselves and we get a sense of self. We exist and there are other beings around us, but they are not us. If we understand this general idea, we begin to experience autonomy. If not, shame is the result.

Stage 3 Preschool 3-5 years: Initiative vs. Guilt

Here not only do I exist, I can impact my environment. I am growing and figuring out this world I am placed in. If I can feel me and initiate in this world, I have a sense of initiative. If not, I begin to experience guilt.

Stage 4 School Age 6-12: Industry vs. Inferiority

Here my world has just gotten way bigger. Now, it's not just my parents, siblings, and significant others in my life, it's a lot of others my size (or close). These other children have different strengths and experiences than I do. If I navigate this bigger world effectively, I have industry and as a result I believe "I can." If I don't navigate successfully here, I come out feeling and believing I'm inferior with a message of "I can't."

Stage 5 Adolescence 12-18: Identity vs. Role Confusion

In this stage, I not only have to continue to maintain my home relationships, I have to continue to navigate the competitive school environment and the task of education. We also need to throw in body changes and hormones and possible romantic/sexual desires, the Internet, or experiences. If I navigate this well, I have a sense of who I am (identity). If I am less successful in navigating all of these tasks and relationships, I come out with role confusion, as I am not clear on who I am.

Stage 6 Early Adulthood 18 -35: Intimacy vs. Isolation

In this stage there is training, college, working, family relationships, sexuality, marriage for many, and starting a career and family. If I know who I am, I can successfully give myself to a marriage or long term relationship. If I don't navigate all of this well, I will pull away from others, and could possibly medicate my life in some manner.

Stage 7 Middle Adulthood 35-55: Generativity vs. Stagnation

If marriage and children have occurred in this stage, you're in the middle of being stretched and matured in many different directions. If not, you're maturing in your career (or areas of interest) and becoming proficient. If you are navigating well, you have a desire to give back to the community and make the world a better place.

Stage 8 Late Adulthood 55 to Death: Integrity vs. Despair

If integrity has occurred, most likely the marriage is present and stable. Your children are starting to leave the nest, and you are able to focus on things that give personal meaning and fulfillment. This person looks at their life and generally feels good about it. If this stage is not navigated well, this person most likely has multiple regrets, and may still be immature in their relationships, as well as other areas of their life. When they assess the quality of their life, they may feel loss and depression.

Let's briefly review these areas of development, both in terms of building from trust or mistrust. A person who builds from trust looks like this:

Trust
Autonomy
Initiative

Industry
Identity
Intimacy
Generativity
Integrity

A person who experienced mistrust in infancy and builds from mistrust looks like this:

Mistrust
Shame
Guilt
Inferiority
Role confusion
Isolation
Stagnation
Despair

Human Development Theory basically believes as we develop (unless there is an intervention), we could naturally progress in these two major directions.

Trauma

When a significant trauma occurs, whether it is PTSD from seeing your friend blown up from a grenade, witnessing a murder, experiencing sexual abuse or rape, partner betrayal trauma, or financial trauma, it is outside the normal realm of human experience.

Although there are unique and different types of trauma, they all have this *outside of the normal range of experience* common denominator. Let's suppose the average daily experience of life provides 40-90 volts of electricity. The body, soul, and spirit generally accept this level of voltage as normal and acceptable.

Then let's say you literally get hit by lightning and your body, soul, and spirit are overwhelmed with a ton of volts of electricity. I actually know someone who was struck by lightning. This experience is so overwhelming, your entire system is taken back to a very primitive survival place. This is where a primitive choice in my opinion is reset, or reestablished.

Trauma is so challenging to the entire human being, because all systems (all at once) experience excruciating pain and the entire system becomes overwhelmed.

I have seen partners of betrayal trauma that were calm, mature, and coherent as we did marital counseling to develop questions for her husband's polygraph. She would also be normal in her individual session relaying her story to me. Then this same woman would come back into the session and I would review his polygraph.

She would receive the truth about infidelity, the number of incidents, the type of infidelity, the last time it happened, and sometimes with who the infidelity occurred. She would receive the truth about his lying about porn, masturbation, or other secrets and the lightning bolt of trauma hits her entire being. This once calm and mature woman is screaming like an animal, convulsing on the floor with her body jerking uncontrollably.

I have seen the lightning bolt of trauma hit women so many times that I find it painful to write about. I recall woman after woman being traumatized by the truth of what her husband or significant other did. What I am trying to share with you is that trauma takes you back to a place of total reset.

Let me change trauma examples to illustrate this. I met a male intimacy anorexic/sex addict client who reported to me that he had great childhood up to age eight. He trusted, developed autonomy and initiative and moved successfully into industry up to this point in his life. At age eight, he was regularly sexually abused by a female for about four to five years.

The sexual trauma totally reset him. This man was a 52-year-old successful accountant when I showed him Erikson's developmental model. He looked at me and said, "That's me. I don't trust anyone." He was able to see how his life took the path of mistrust since that point of the trauma. He reset to mistrust. He was able to identify with every single stage from mistrust to despair in his life development.

I met a beautiful and smart 45-year-old female client who had a great childhood up to age twelve. She also experienced trust, autonomy, initiative, and industry in her family of origin. She was set up into a rape situation at age 12. When I showed her Erikson's development model, she also quickly identified with the mistrust side and said exactly the same thing, "I don't trust anyone." Her trauma also carried a reset.

To be fair, neither of these people were old enough to have abstract reasoning (ages 8 and 12) to be able to navigate these traumas. Both people would have been in stages with concrete thinking with the mindset, "Bad things happen to bad people therefore, I must be bad."

Trauma can also reset a person in the other direction. I live in a military town where it is common to see a man or woman who lost a limb through a traumatic military experience. They may have never trusted anyone, or experienced initiative, industry, identity, or intimacy prior to the trauma. The trauma recovery demanded this soldier trust his medical team or physical therapist and this moved the soldier right up the chain from trusting authority, initiative, industry, identity, and intimacy. This soldier can go on to create a full life which might include participating in sports. The trauma causes a reset.

Partner Betrayal Trauma Reset

As a partner of betrayal trauma, you have experienced the full-on voltage of trauma affecting all areas of your being. Your trauma also provides a reset opportunity that can and will affect the rest of your life.

> "YOUR TRAUMA ALSO PROVIDES A RESET OPPORTUNITY THAT CAN AND WILL AFFECT THE REST OF YOUR LIFE."

I have worked one-on-one with thousands of partners of betrayal over the last 30 years of my life. I have seen the impact of resets to mistrust. Here are some variables involved in the reset process with partners of betrayal trauma.

General/Specific

When trauma occurs, you have to process the trauma in some way. When you start processing this trauma it is easy to generalize your pain with thinking "all men are liars, cheaters, addicts, sick, just want sex, whores, dogs, and so on." However, when a woman generalizes her pain to all men, she can reset to mistrust in her life.

The betrayal may involve other woman or several women you know. Woman to woman betrayal is a painful experience if the woman is a friend, family member, in-law, acquaintance, coworker, employee, or in some way familiar to you. Woman to woman betrayal is huge and is often never discussed, or addressed by therapists.

Again, if a woman generalizes "all women cheat, lie, want money, and are whores" she could reset to mistrust. This mistrust reset could last for an indefinite period of time.

A woman, who for whatever reason generalizes her betrayal, will often reset to mistrust. She may be motivated by fear, or a need to feel safe. If this is short-term, she won't totally reset down the less than positive developmental path. If she stays in this position, she can reset to mistrust and move her life down this path because of this reset.

Remember, resets happen in the primitive state as you experience trauma. You may not be aware that you reset to mistrust, but your behavior after the trauma event will show you if it has occurred.

The other option for processing trauma is to make it specific to the person who caused it. Your husband or significant other betrayed you. In that moment he forfeited all good judgement, acted immaturely, selfishly, and even destructively. He alone is your perpetrator.

If another woman was involved and she had a relationship with your spouse or significant other, she alone chose to betray you and your relationship by acting selfishly, recklessly, and irresponsibly.

The woman who processes betrayal trauma this way, may have all kinds of feelings and words to describe her husband or significant other. This woman will also believe and behave that there are good men who will never do this. They will trust other men in their family, male friends, and even men who are professionals. This woman will also believe there are good women and remain trusting in these relationships.

Centric/Decentric

Remember the two sexual abuse resets I gave you earlier? In both cases, the individuals did not have abstract reasoning so they couldn't process trauma in the specific manner we just discussed. They brought the trauma back to themselves to process (centric) concluding that somehow, they are to blame for the trauma happening to them. This is a very centric way of processing pain because the event/pain is about me.

If an adult woman (who does have abstract reasoning), processes trauma in a centric way she will regularly be drawn back to ideas that it is about her. He did X, Y, and Z behaviors because, "I am not enough, I am fat, not good in bed, old, ugly, bad at housekeeping, not good with money, not fun, or not fit."

She will also process when he did X, Y, Z, behavior, "He hated me, he didn't love me, he was rejecting me, my love, my sex, and my beauty." The more centric she processes the trauma the longer this processing can take, because these beliefs are not the total truth, or possibly not true at all.

The centric process woman doesn't just distrust him, she can't trust herself, her judgement, her real reason for staying, others, and professionals. She is more likely to reset toward mistrust.

When a woman is able to process the pain of the trauma and give him 100% of the responsibility, she processes the betrayal differently and quicker than her centric counterpart. This woman says, "He is immature, selfish, maybe addicted or anorexic and this is why he chose X, Y, Z. No matter who he married he would have done these things."

This woman has decentralized the betrayal. He did this, it

had nothing to do with me. This woman is not likely to reset toward mistrust at all. I have women tell me clearly, "I am an awesome wife, I am great and creative in bed, smart, and I make good money. He did this because he is stupid. He has one chance to grow up, or I'm out."

While the trauma can be exactly the same for each of these women, the way they process the betrayal makes the difference in how a woman resets.

Stagnant vs Neoplastic

The other observation that can affect a trauma reset is the belief the woman has about growth in general.

If a woman has a more stagnant perception of life, she likes everything to stay the same, and she doesn't like change or taking risks. She generally doesn't demand much of herself physically, emotionally, and socially and stays in the same circle and generally moves toward "sameness."

This person would have challenges experiencing any trauma. Trauma, including partner betrayal trauma, takes you way outside of your normal life. You might be faced with so many changes, so quickly, that it challenges your core beliefs about yourself—your worth, capability, and adaptability.

> "TRAUMA, INCLUDING PARTNER BETRAYAL TRAUMA, TAKES YOU WAY OUTSIDE OF YOUR NORMAL LIFE."

I have seen women lose their husband, home, and financial security, seek employment (with little skills), change schools for their children, and try to heal from the betrayal—all at the same time.

As you can see, someone who has a stagnant perspective or lifestyle will impact the process and speed of recovering from trauma. This can also impact how they reset. Mistrust is easier up front (with less risk), for the person with a stagnant perspective.

Neuroplastic

The neuroplastic perspective is one of growth, change, and learning as a normal lifestyle. This woman has a history of growing and learning in several areas of her life (over her lifetime). She believes "she can" pretty much learn, grow, and change at will.

This woman engages life and relationships and is usually achieving some goal in her life. She (at her core), believes change is part of life. She believes she is neuroplastic and can grow, adapt, change, and discipline herself to achieve the adaptations of choice.

Her neuroplastic core beliefs play a significant role in how she processes trauma. She expresses the pain, grief, thoughts, and feelings like all women. She asks the following questions: "How do I heal?" "What's the process?" "What books should I read?" "Who are the best professionals?"

This woman tends to move toward the process and relationships to adapt in a healthy way. She usually trusts in support groups or therapy, allowing her to process pain, but not stay in the pain or victim place. She is more likely to reset toward trust, with a team of new women to help her heal from partner betrayal.

As you read through all of this, my hope is you will see where you are in the reset process. Your awareness of this could radically change your process of healing.

You can't change the fact that you have been betrayed and lied to often and many times over many years—that's the trauma piece. The betrayal piece is yours to process and heal from. That part is up to you.

> "THE BETRAYAL PIECE IS YOURS TO PROCESS AND HEAL FROM."

10

Responsibility

In working with partners of betrayal trauma one of the issues that comes up is responsibility. I agree this is a very important issue, and I want to discuss it generally (and then specifically).

First, I want to remind you of the founding principles I have discussed for decades in my treatment of partners. These are the same principles I use to instruct any therapist, coach, or minister who wants to get certified as a PRT (Partners Recovery Therapist) through the American Association of Sex Addiction Therapy (AASAT).

1. Every partner is absolutely unique and worthy of honor for whom they presently are.
2. The partner has no responsibility for the addict's addiction or acting out.
3. Partners come anywhere on the continuum of spiritual, emotional, physical, financial, sexual, and social health.
4. Any partner who takes responsibility for herself can heal and grow in areas she deems necessary.

5. The addiction often creates collateral damage that is best to heal from as early as possible.

6. There are no core beliefs or attributes for partners. They are all unique beings.

I think it is clear he is 100% responsible for his infidelity, sex addiction, behavior with self and others, pornography, or intimacy anorexia withholding behaviors. He would have made immature decisions and done this, regardless of who he married or chose to be with in a romantic relationship. All behavior is 100% his responsibility, period.

His behavior wasn't because you were not enough, or because of your weight, height, size of any part of you, wrinkles, gray hair, or something about your past, or personality. He made decisions 100% based upon who he was in those moments.

His choices absolutely 100% caused your trauma. It will take him time in recovery, and being truly sober from whatever his behavior was, until he might fully accept his responsibility for the betrayal. However, you and I are perfectly clear he is responsible for the betrayal and the nuances of impact on all the lives he impacted.

Having said all this, let me move right into what he is responsible for. I find (early on) this connection can be helpful to keep expectations reasonable.

<u>His Responsibility</u>

1. He is responsible to give you a voluntary disclosure (if you want to know) of the following:

   A. What the behaviors were (porn, masturbation, other people, strip clubs, prostitutes, etc.)

B. When it started in your relationship and when was the last time
C. Approximately, or as close as he can know, the number of people involved
D. The last communication, in any format with the people his behavior involved
    i. Here I would seek counseling. Getting very detailed information can hurt you very much for a long time (positions, places, what was said). You will never forget those things and they can become hurdles in your healing. Seriously consider that no detail will heal you. If you want to create a list of detailed questions, do so, then go to a specialist in this area before you demand more information.

E. He can take a polygraph (early on) to verify the facts of this general disclosure after discovery
F. He can take quarterly polygraphs to verify he is staying free from behaviors and communications of past people and not grooming anyone in the present

2. He can equip himself to help you in your healing process by watching *Helping Her Heal* (DVD). He can practice the "Understanding Her" exercise about 20 times with you so he can be there for you when you are in legitimate pain or being triggered early in recovery.

3. He can work a solid recovery plan for himself which might include:

    A. Reading material like: *The Final Freedom* book, *101 Freedom Exercises Workbook*, and *Steps to Freedom-Workbook*.
    B. Read books to help him understand your experience *Partners: Healing from His Addiction* and *Partners Recovery Guide Workbook*)
    C. Attend support groups

D. He won't heal by himself
E. Go to individual/marriage counseling or 3- and 5-Day Intensives to facilitate his healing

4. He can keep his word on small and large responsibilities, or issues.

5. He can stop lying and set a consequence for himself if he does lie.

6. He can build a team of accountability with other recovery men that he calls regularly.

7. He can grow spiritually.

8. He can share his feelings with you.

<u>What He Can't Do</u>

1. He can't remove the past mistakes, or the pain it has caused you and your family.

2. He can't mature and be a real adult man initially, especially if he's a sex addict or intimacy anorexic. He will mature, but it can take up to a year before you feel you're living with a mature adult emotionally.

3. He can't make you feel safe, or any other feeling for that matter. I recommend the DVD *I Need to Feel Safe* to help you heal.

4. He cannot "make" you trust again. This is a two-sided journey. He can become trustworthy, but trust will still need to be given at some point.

5. He cannot be your support person. Early on, he will be immature. You will want an adult woman who can be there for you in your healing process.

6. He cannot stabilize you emotionally. You will need wom-

en to help here and I recommend the book *Emotional Fitness* to strengthen emotional regulation during this period of healing for both of you.

Your Responsibility

Your trauma is like being in a car accident that you didn't cause. You were shot by someone who said they would protect you. He can grow and change if he chooses. However, regardless of his choices about you, or the relationship, you are responsible to heal yourself from the trauma.

> "REGARDLESS OF HIS CHOICES ABOUT YOU, OR THE RELATIONSHIP, YOU ARE RESPONSIBLE TO HEAL YOURSELF FROM THE TRAUMA."

You have incurred several layers and dynamics of pain to work through. You will go through healing at your own pace and unique manner because your trauma is unique to you.

I have helped thousands of partners of betrayal trauma reclaim their lives, regardless of his choices. Your healing and future from this trauma will be totally your responsibility.

Here is some general guidance on what you are responsible for to be as successful as you can be.

1. You are neuroplastic in every aspect of your life, so you can grow, adapt, change, and heal. It will require work, but healing is possible. Believing that healing is possible is very important. Your beliefs about healing is a great resource, or hinderance, to the healing process. You are responsible for what you believe.

2. You will have to evaluate any "meaning" you give to his

behavior and believe meaning that gives 100% responsibility to him for his choices.

3. You will have to choose a path of recovery that is more than just partner betrayal trauma. Identifying and healing the trauma piece is significant and important, but not complete for partners. If he is a sex addict, or intimacy anorexic, I strongly suggest the *Partners Recovery Guide* and the *Married and Alone Workbook* for a more complete approach to your healing. I believe this is a both/and, not an either/or issue in partner recovery.

4. A solid recovery for you will look like:
   A. Support groups (phone or in person)
   B. Making calls to other women regularly
   C. Working through materials (*Partner Betrayal Trauma Workbook*, and *Partner Betrayal Steps Workbook* would be a good start)
   D. Growing spiritually

5. Assess and address the physical impact on your body from the trauma and create an action plan to heal.

6. Exercise and eat well to provide optimal conditions for healing to take place.

7. Genuinely accept your powerlessness over him, his choices, his recovery, or the future (working the 12-Step Workbook can help here).

8. Do not overly focus on his recovery (have weekly check-ins, or every other week where you both check in on your recovery).

9. Find a specialized counselor who you trust to help you process painful issues and help you determine if your behaviors are appropriate or reasonable.

10. Create a team of people who are available to you (at least for the first year) to help you heal.

11. Avoid mistrust of others. While it is true that he and maybe some others violated you, keep your heart open to trust others so you can move forward in your healing.

12. Love yourself and make sure you maintain consistent self-care.

I have learned quite bit over the years about partner betrayal trauma. I have seen women crash and burn their entire lives. They lost their jobs and their families rejected them. For decades, these women wouldn't get help, they stayed angry, bitter, and resentful for what he did to her and they never really managed to heal. These are tragic situations and sadly they do occur. This woman remains the victim and won't reach out to heal, or be open to the fact that her thinking has become impaired.

I have also seen women who have experienced significant trauma from their spouse that move on to have a better life than before (sexually, spiritually, emotionally, financially, and with family and friends). These women even have better marriages if he does the work of recovery. I have seen women brave the storm of divorce and health consequences, come out strong, making great choices. They were sad about his choices, but these women did not take responsibility, or give false meaning to his poor choices, and completely moved on and healed.

The difference between these women is found in classical literature. Let me share with you the two major types of fictional literature that reflects real life. You know there is a main character. She is special in some way. She might be brilliant, a daughter of a king, a warrior, or socialite. She gets lost, rejected, or experienced some tragedy or pain. She is found, or she searches for a solution. She finds a person, mentor, magical being, or tribe that introduces her to new ideas and the solution to whatever her real problem is.

Right here, both forms of classical literature stay the same. You don't know if you are reading a tragedy, or a hero epic. The next chapter tells you the difference. In the tragedy, the heroine doesn't apply what she was taught, won't try, won't get up, won't resist the nemesis with all her heart, or is killed trying. It's this lack of applying what she has learned that causes the tragedy.

On the other hand, there is the hero epic. Hero epics make up most of American movies. The heroine has the same background as the heroine that failed. She integrates her new experiences and learns from those ahead of her in this tribe, and she finds herself. She feels her pain, grieves her losses, fights with all she has, and defeats the disease, the nemesis, solves the problem, and conquers what she needs to.

Your story is 100% your responsibility. You're not responsible for what has been thrust on you by your spouse or significant other. However, now the pen is in your hand. You write your story. My hope and sincere prayer is for you to write an amazing hero epic, so those watching see you become the awesome woman you were meant to be!

"YOUR STORY IS 100% YOUR RESPONSIBILITY. YOU'RE NOT RESPONSIBLE FOR WHAT HAS BEEN THRUST ON YOU BY YOUR SPOUSE OR SIGNIFICANT OTHER."

11

The Twelve Steps

1. We admitted we were powerless over the betrayal from our spouse/significant other—that our lives had become unmanageable.

2. Came to believe that a Power greater than ourselves could restore us to sanity.

3. Made a decision to turn our will and our lives over to the care of God as we understood Him.

4. Made a searching and fearless moral inventory of ourselves.

5. Admitted to God, to ourselves, and to another human being the exact nature of our wrongs.

6. Were entirely ready to have God remove all these defects of character.

7. Humbly asked Him to remove our shortcomings.

8. Made a list of all people we had harmed, and became willing to make amends to them all.

9. Made direct amends to such people wherever possible, except when to do so would injure them or others.

10. Continued to take personal inventory, and when we were wrong, promptly admitted it.

11. Sought through prayer and meditation to improve our conscious contact with God as we understood Him, praying only for knowledge of His will for us and the power to carry that out.

12. Having had a spiritual awakening as the result of these steps, we tried to carry this message to others, and to practice these principles in all our affairs.

Note: The Twelve Steps are reprinted and adapted with permission of Alcoholics Anonymous World Services, Inc. Permission to reprint and adapt the Twelve Steps does not mean that AA has reviewed or approved the content of this publication, nor that AA agrees with the views expressed herein. AA is a program of recovery from alcoholism. Use of the Twelve Steps in connection with programs and activities which are patterned after AA, but which address other problems, does not imply otherwise.

An Interpretation of the Twelve Steps

What we will attempt to do in the following pages is explain the principles and concepts of the Twelve Steps as they are used in recovery for partners of betrayal trauma, so you can implement them in your personal recovery. The comments here should not be construed as representing any particular Twelve Step fellowship. They are my own interpretation of the Twelve Steps from my own experience, as well as from years of clinical experience helping partners of betrayal trauma recover by using the Twelve Step process.

1

WE ADMITTED WE WERE POWERLESS OVER THE BETRAYAL FROM OUR SPOUSE/SIGNIFICANT OTHER—THAT OUR LIVES HAD BECOME UNMANAGEABLE.

We. I am so glad that the first word in the first step is "we." I would hate to think I was the only person who ever went through the pain of being betrayed by their spouse or significant other. Being a partner of betrayal trauma is a national, as well as an international problem. "We" means that we have similar experiences and we share similarities. We have experienced similar trauma. I think the chapters you have read validate your similarities to other partners. The word "we" is a comforting word in this step. You can see that you are not alone and don't have to be alone. You can get better if you decide to get together. While "we" is an encouraging word it is also essential. Without each other, we often fail to recover from the effects of partner betrayal trauma. Here is where we can trust other women to heal.

Admitted. This is a difficult word. Many of us have had situations in our childhood that we have had to admit. Maybe we stole something, or something happened to us, and we had to admit what we did. Do you remember those feelings of dread before admitting to something? Then we went ahead and admitted it. We told what we did or what happened to us. After we admitted it, we felt less heavy or burdened as if we could now move on. Admitting to the effects from his betrayal (and now our own trauma), is one of the more difficult things we will do in our recovery. Admitting is a very important aspect of recovery. Only those who admit to being hurt can move forward in recovery and life. You have been betrayed, and that is sadly a fact in your healing.

We Were Powerless. Again, I'm glad that there is a "we" here. I'm not the only one who is powerless. When we talk about power, we talk about control. Authority, strength, or force gives us the ability to control someone else. But that is not what this word is. This word is powerless and as we know, the suffix "less" means without (like jobless). This is a tough reality for every partner. We are without any strength, power, control, or force to influence our betrayal, or the trauma it caused in our life. This is why we need each other and a recovery program. Sometimes that is why we need therapy. We are powerless.

Our Betrayal. Being powerless over our betrayal is difficult. You have experienced betrayal. Your body, soul, spirit, sexuality, your relationships—all of you—is impacted by the poor choices of your husband or significant other.

You had nothing to do with his choices. However, healing from the trauma of his betrayal is your unique journey. Accepting this factual betrayal of his is part of the journey for your recovery.

Our Spouse or Significant Other. The one who said I will forsake all others and love, honor, and cherish you is the person who committed the betrayal in your life. This is the unique variable among all other traumas. He is the one who promised that you could be eternally safe with him, and he is the one who chose to betrayal you.

This is sadly a fact whether he chose infidelity, sex addiction, or intimacy anorexia. He chose to betray you. This is why this trauma is unique, and why you were powerless to prevent it from entering your life.

And That Our Lives. Our lives can be many things. It can be our physical, emotional, intellectual, or spiritual life. If you look at all the parts of our lives, they wouldn't equal the totality of our life. Our lives are the very core of us. It is the inner part of us that identifies us as being separate from another person. This is what has been impacted as we look at the effects of the betrayal trauma.

Had Become. These two words indicate to me that this has taken a while. It means that it took time, energy, a process, and choices. It didn't just happen. It took a while and then eventually, it was made. Your life didn't become overwhelming or devastated instantly, but over a period of time. His betrayal is multidimensional and multifaceted over a period of time.

Unmanageable. When we think about manageable, we think about things being in order, or serene. We can tell when we walk into a store whether the store is manageable or unmanageable. Unmanageable means unorganized and chaotic. If someone came from the outside and saw this, they would say, "What a mess!" Sometimes this is the way we feel, and our feelings can be valid. Our lives, in many of the areas we have talked about, have become unmanageable, unconnected, uncontrollable, and unpredictable. No matter how hard we have tried to make our lives look good or perfect, they are not. Our lives have become empty and hollow in many respects. Now through Step One, if we can admit this unmanageability, we have a strong hope of recovery.

I encourage everyone to take Step One seriously, because it is the foundation of the Twelve Step program. It will cause you to have a good house of recovery to live in for the future.

For further step work on Step One and all of the Twelve Steps for partners, I encourage you to use the workbook *Partner Betrayal Trauma Steps* workbook for general or the

Partner Betrayal Trauma Exercise workbook. These guides are designed specifically for partners. These are available through Heart to Heart Counseling Center and can be ordered at www.drougweiss.com or www.sexaddict.com.

2

CAME TO BELIEVE THAT A POWER GREATER THAN OURSELVES COULD RESTORE US TO SANITY.

Came to Believe. Again, notice the step is written in the past tense. The original steps were written to share the process that the original members of Alcoholics Anonymous (AA) went through in recovery. There was a process through which they came to believe.

It is really a simple process. You come to believe many things during your lifetime. For example, at some point in your life you probably came to believe that there was a Santa Claus. Later, you came to believe that there wasn't a Santa Claus. As you grew older, you might have come to believe that a certain person liked you and later realized they didn't like you. You come to believe certain religious and political positions. There is some consistency to this process throughout our lives. In this process there is a definite point at which you understand (or come to believe).

In Twelve Step groups, the process of *coming to believe* is something that often happens as a result of exposure to other recovering people. You may not necessarily know the date, or the hour, when you did come to believe, but you know that you felt different, and you began to have hope. This is so important in recovery, because knowing that you have come to believe, or knowing you do believe can save your life. Partners can get down, feel hopeless, worthless, experience severe guilt and shame from past traumas, or present circumstances, and resort to sad behaviors of destruction, isolation, or depression. If you come to believe, you have hope.

A Power. "A" is a common word. You use it every day. A cat, a dog, a book and in every context in which it is used, it denotes one. If you were going to use a word to describe more than one, you would say "these," or another word that indicates plurality. This step is not written in the plural. It says "a" Power greater than ourselves. This is significant. Having an "a" here, you realize that there is one entity, one strength, one energy, one spirit, one Power. It is significant that, as you come to believe, you are believing in One being.

Greater Than Ourselves. This is one of the first areas which requires trust from the partner. We now know that there is One that is greater than ourselves. This is the best news we have in recovery that we don't have to figure this out alone. As you begin to trust this Power, you begin to recover from the sick patterns, poor choices, and undesirable relationships that have been so much a part of your past.

In the original context of AA, this Power greater than ourselves indicates that the Power was greater than that first group of recovering alcoholics. This one single Power was greater than a whole group. That's a lot of power. People in recovery frequently first recognize this Power in the group, but in reality, it is greater than the group. Even if you had a Power greater than yourself, you may have had difficulty accessing the resources of that Power and applying them to your life. In the program, you come to believe that this Power has more ability to solve life's problems than you do alone. What a relief!

Could. Could is one of the most helpful, loving expressions in the Twelve Steps. Could this Power have the ability, the resources, the energy, the intention of helping you along in the recovery process? It is possible now to begin to be restored even from partner betrayal trauma. It is possible now to begin to be healthy, to have loving relationships with loving people, to be loved and nurtured in a healthy way. It can be done, and this Power can do it. It is the experience of many partners in recovery that, given the freedom and opportunity, if you quit trying to do it all on your own, this Power will do for you what you have been unable, or unwilling to do for yourself. All you have to do is ask.

Restore Us to Sanity. Restore means bringing something back. Frequently when you think of restoration, you think of restoring an automobile or an old house, making it look like new. The same is true for those recovering from the effects of betrayal trauma.

Partners have for so long been robbed of spirituality, intimacy, trust, and even their own reality. In a world that should have been safe, you were violated again and again.

Insanity is natural when you live with someone who chooses to betray you. You may have difficulty applying the idea of insanity to yourself. However, having two realities at the same time, and living with the secret, can make most partners feel insane. You try again and again to do something that should work, but it doesn't. You try and try to fix the problems that his choices and your trauma creates in your life, without success.

The behaviors themselves are not insane, but the fact that you continue to use them without stopping to realize that they're not working, qualifies you to be restored to sanity. It is possible for partners of betrayal trauma to be restored to sanity. Those already in recovery have experienced it. They are living proof that it is possible to make better choices, and we hope as you read this, you know that it is possible for you. You may still feel crazy, but if you have gotten this far in your recovery, you have a good chance of finding sanity.

3

MADE A DECISION TO TURN OUR WILL AND OUR LIVES OVER TO THE CARE OF GOD AS WE UNDERSTOOD HIM.

Made. Made is like the word "become" which indicates a process that involves time and choices, but there is definitely a time when it is done. For example, when kids in school make an ashtray, a meal, or a dress in home economics, or a table in shop, there is a time when it is in the process of being made, and then it is completed. It is made.

Made is something that has been coming along but is finally resolved to the point that you can say it is done.

A. Here again we come to that little word "a" indicating it is one. What we are discussing in Step Three is a onetime event. Many people want to spread this step out, but as you move along in this process of working the Twelve Steps, you will see why we only make this decision one time.

Decision. When you make a decision, you list the good and the bad, the pros and cons, of a situation. In this step, you make a list of what you have done with your life in the past, and how you could deal with your life differently in the future. Such a list makes it easier to make the decision you are asked to make in Step Three. It is a decision.

Compare it to a traditional courtship and marriage. In Step Two you had an engagement period, during which you get to know your Power greater than yourself, and you began to get comfortable with the idea of having God in your life.

Step Three is the marriage ceremony itself, where you make a commitment to share your life with God. You have a single ceremony, but it sets the stage for further development through the relationship. Step Three asks you to be willing to share your life with God. The decision is a onetime event, but it provides a means for further growth.

To Turn. Turning can be expressed in many ways. Someone once said that turning means to flip over, like a hotcake. The hotcake gets done on one side, and then you have to turn it over.

This is a pretty simple definition of turn, but it is also pretty profound. If you flip over, you make a total change from the way you have been up to this point. "Turn" is used on highways all over the world to indicate direction. These signs may indicate a left or right turn, or a U-turn. When you make a U-turn, you turn around and go in the opposite direction. What you do in Step Three is definitely a U-turn! You turn away from your limited understanding of how life should be. You leave behind perceptions, experiences, and ideas about things you thought you understood. You turn from them and gain a whole new perspective. This is an essential part of recovery. You are turning into something, or turning somewhere else, and it is amazing how far that turn can take you as you continue in your recovery efforts.

Our Will. Again, our will is plural, as the group stays and works together. In this group of safe people (who have turned their wills and lives over to God), you begin to see this decision as a possibility for yourself. But what is your will? The simplest definition of will is the ability to make choices for your life. In the group, you will begin to turn over the choices that you make to God. This can be an easy thing for some, but for others it can be a very hard thing to do. It means you must turn your choices over to God, try to understand God's perspective, and follow that perspective in your life. That is why Step Three is so powerful.

In many recovery groups there is a phrase called "stinking thinking" which refers to dysfunctional thought patterns that addicts often have. Stinking thinking is the way a non-recovering person thinks. This thinking doesn't work. The choices non-recovering people make don't bring about positive results. There seems to be certain self-destructiveness to their choices and behavior. Step Three cuts to the core of stinking thinking. It is the beginning of a new lifestyle.

Giving up our will is a safety valve. In making decisions about relationships, we are now able to turn to God. As we do, God will show us new directions we can take and new choices we can make. We begin getting answers and are able make different choices about our relationships. This is a freedom that is only gained by letting go of our will, or sharing the responsibility of choosing with God.

Our Lives. Our lives are the result of all our choices. For each individual, life is the totality of all parts (spiritual, physical, social, financial, and sexual). When you turn over every area of your life you give yourself to God and you begin to trust Him. You begin to believe that God will take care of you.

You may say, "This is frightening! How can I trust God?" But simply look at what you have trusted in the past. You have trusted your own ability to think and your own ability to make choices. You have taken the advice of a few chosen people who have not necessarily acted in your best interests.

Turning over your will and your life is necessary. It is through this trust experience with God, that you begin to believe that God loves you. You begin once again to trust yourself. Eventually, you can even regain your trust in people. Step Three is an essential part of working the Twelve Steps. It is not a luxury. It is necessary for a healthy, happy life. Working the Twelve Steps is not always easy, and often you do not understand why you must work them. Often the Twelve Steps are understood only after they have been completed. Then you realize the beauty of this spiritual process, and open yourself to further growth and joy, as you walk this road with others who are making the same steps toward recovery.

The Care of God. What do you think of when you hear the word care? Care is often expressed in terms of someone who loves you, someone who demonstrates some kindness toward you, or someone who is willing to get involved in your life. This person is willing to get in there, be patient with you, work with you, and not condemn you in the process, someone who is nurturing. All these pictures of a loving parent, or a loving friend represent care. Care is felt in the release of energy from one person to another, usually through kind behaviors, like providing a listening ear, or some other sign of concern.

How does this relate to God? What is the care of God? It is simply God's willingness to be involved in a nurturing, supportive, accepting way in your life. God is concerned for partners. God's concern for others in this world demonstrates that care. You can sometimes see it more clearly in the lives of others, than you can in your own life. For some partners, the group is a manifestation of the care of God in their lives. It is possible for you, by looking at others in your support group, to connect with this issue in such a way that it radically changes your life. Something as simple as their support can be seen as the extension of God's care and concern.

Now, we'll talk about God. The original writers of the Twelve Steps changed only one word from their initial version. In Step Two, they changed the word "God" to "a Power greater than ourselves." That is the only change they made, and it was made for this reason: those first alcoholics said that God was too scary for the recovering person in Step Two. Maybe the recovering person had too many hurts, too many problems with God, so the word was changed to "a Power greater than ourselves." This gave the newcomer an engagement period, to allow him or her to experience God through the group's care, nurturing, and love. In this way they could come to believe in a caring God who could and would help them.

But who is God? Let me share my thoughts with you on this subject. Simply put, God is Love. God is also in authority, or in control, especially for those who turn their lives and their will over to Him, switching authority from ourselves to God.

According to what you have learned so far in the Twelve Steps, God has the ability to restore you. God is more powerful than you are alone, or in a group. God is one who gets actively involved in your life, one who has more power, and more success than you. This God can and will, help you as you work the Twelve Steps. For many, this understanding of God will develop into a faith that is common in American culture and will enable the recovering partner to enjoy the benefits of finding a community that shares a similiar faith. Some will not. It is a universal blessing of this program, however, that they can (if they are willing), to come to a greater relationship with God, as they understand Him.

Those who turn their will and lives over to the care of a God they understand, often have more understanding of how God works and how God thinks. The group is a good resource, especially for those early in recovery who want an understanding of God. It is very important to realize (as it pertains to understanding God), that no single person is going to understand the totality of God. However, the members of your support group can be helpful in this journey.

As We Understood Him. One way to interpret this is to compare your understanding of God with the way you function in relationships with people, because we are talking about a relationship. When you first meet someone, your knowledge of them is limited. Only through time, communication, and commitment in any relationship, do you really come to understand another person. The same is true in your relationship with God. Coming to understand God is a process which is available to any and all in recovery. Those who are willing to turn their will and lives over will experience a new life, new freedom, and find happiness. This is the beauty of finding God in the Twelve Steps.

4

MADE A SEARCHING AND FEARLESS MORAL INVENTORY OF OURSELVES.

Made A Searching. Searching holds the possibility of fun, but for partners, searching can be extremely painful. When you search you intend to find something you are looking for. For example, when you lose your keys, you go searching with the intent of finding the keys. As you begin your inventory, you search, scrutinize, and seek with intent to find something significant.

In this context, searching indicates that you will have to expend some energy. This is the beginning of what is often referred to in the program as "action steps." You now begin to take action on your own behalf. Note that this step is also in the past tense. As you begin your inventory, you can know that others have passed this way before, they survived and got better. You are not alone.

Fearless. Fearless simply means without fear. This is the attitude with which you approach your moral inventory. Being fearless allows you to view your inventory objectively, as you uncover the pain. You will be looking at what was done to you, and what you have done to yourself, and others.

Many of the experiences you will be looking at are extremely painful. For some, the painful experience was childhood abuse. Others may have experienced abuse or neglect, including their relationship with the person who betrayed them. For some, it will be something they would much rather forget, something they may think they only imagined. Fearlessness will lead you to look at your own part in the unhealthy relationships you have been in as an adult, and at the patterns that have been repeated in your life. You need to look at these things with an attitude of courage and bravery. You can, because in Step Three you turned your will and life over to the care of a loving God.

Moral. Moral can be defined as right and wrong, categories of black and white, or good and bad. Something that is immoral could be defined as something that violates your conscience. As you look at your life in Step Four, you will be looking for things you've done that have violated your conscience. For example, as children many of us had the experience of raiding the cookie jar. We knew that we were not supposed to get a cookie. There might not be anything wrong with having a cookie, but we were told not to so it was wrong. We waited until our parents could not see and took a cookie anyway. It probably tasted good but we may have felt bad afterward. We felt bad because we knew we did something wrong.

In Step Four, you will also be looking at how you were violated by others. Have you ever said to yourself, "If they really knew me, they wouldn't like me? If they knew I was sexually abused, or that my partner betrayed me, they wouldn't be my friend." The shame and guilt you carry (from the actions of other people toward you), can be overwhelming. Step Four is designed to release you from that shame and guilt, as you look at how your moral code has been violated by others.

It is wrong to believe that you are unworthy because of your past. In recovery, you come to know yourself and let others know you. Step Four is about coming to know yourself, being honest with yourself about what happened, taking into account how it affected your life, and where it leaves you today. In short, Step Four is an inventory. You will list everything that happened, even if it involved others and you were simply an innocent bystander, as in the case of the divorce of your parents.

Such an event may not have had anything to do with your morality, but it did affect you emotionally.

Inventory. What are you to inventory in Step Four? You inventory your experiences because, as a human being, that is what you have on hand. You inventory your memory, for that is what you have been given to record your experiences. Many see this inventory as a life story. It is a process where you begin to see the truth of what you've done, and what has been done to you. Some things will be negative, others will be positive. When a storekeeper takes inventory, he lists not only the things he wants to get rid of, but the things he wants to keep. And he doesn't just make a mental note, he writes it all down.

Step Four is a written assignment. You will need to have pen or pencil, paper, and a quiet place where you can be uninterrupted. Some just begin writing. Some organize their inventory by ages, such as birth to six years, seven to twelve years, and so on. Still others have done it by first listing all the traumatic events they can remember (things that were done to them, or by them, that violated their value system). Then they write how they felt at the time and how they feel now about those events. There is no right or wrong way to write an inventory. The important thing is just to do it. You will be face-to-face (perhaps for the first time) with the total reality of your life. This process can be pretty overwhelming, so don't be afraid to let your sponsor or therapist know how you are feeling while writing your inventory. As you transfer your story to paper, you are also transferring the pain, guilt, and shame onto paper. Writing an inventory can be a very positive, transforming experience, and it is vital to your recovery from the effects of his betrayal.

Of Ourselves. Once again, "of ourselves" is plural. You can know that others have done this before. You can survive the pain of writing your inventory down. It is joyous to see others freed from their shame. As you see other members of your support groups complete their inventories, you will begin to believe that this release from shame can happen for you too. You are reminded that only you can do this for yourself. Only you know your pain, the strength of your fears, your deepest secrets. Only you are qualified to write this inventory. Now is the time to decide for yourself who you are, and who you want to be. There is great freedom in taking your focus off what is wrong with others and doing a searching and fearless moral inventory of yourself. You may not understand the value of this step until you have completed it, but it is well worth the pain and tears.

5

ADMITTED TO GOD, TO OURSELVES, AND TO ANOTHER HUMAN BEING THE EXACT NATURE OF OUR WRONGS.

Admitted. Here you are again, looking at that word admitted. You already know that it means to fess up or acknowledge what is already true. You may have already experienced the pain and joy of doing this, probably as a child or adolescent. Perhaps you put yourself in a situation you knew your parents wouldn't approve. Or you did something wrong and you knew you were going to have to tell them, because you knew they were going to find out anyway. Do you remember your feelings of guilt and shame, like you had let yourself and them down? Then somehow, you got the courage to tell them what you had done. You admitted the truth, no matter the consequences. It felt better finally to let the secret out.

The same is true in Step Five. You admit all that you have written in Step Four. You let out all those secrets and finally feel that clean joy which comes from truly being totally known.

To God. God might be the easiest person to tell (or the hardest), depending on your relationship with Him. If you feel God has let you down before, admitting what has been wrong in your life can be particularly difficult. Fortunately, God is forgiving of all that you have done, and is willing to restore any lost part of yourself. As one wise person in recovery said, "It's okay to tell God. God already knows it all anyway and He is just waiting for us to be honest about it, too."

To Ourselves. Admitting your past secrets to yourself often takes place as you write your inventory in Step Four, if you are truly fearless and thorough when writing it. Admitting your powerlessness, your need to be restored to sanity, your profound amazement at your poor choices, and your sincere sense of having failed yourself, is probably the most humbling experience you will have regarding your sense of who you are.

It is at this point that the recovery of your true self is able to take an upward turn, without the overwhelming sense of shame or guilt that has been so closely bound to you in the past. You are now able to begin a more shame-free life, which empowers you to experience the next, and most essential part of this step, being able to reveal yourself to another human being.

And to Another Human Being. "What? I have to tell all this stuff to somebody else, face-to-face?" Yes, telling your story to another human being is the most crucial part of your recovery. In writing your story in Step Four, you have taken your total history of shame, hurt, abandonment, abuse, and poor choices, and poured it consciously into one place. Your Fourth Step may even have brought to your consciousness an awareness of some things you have been suppressing for years. Now all of these memories are together in one place. If all this pain is kept inside you and is not shared with another human being, you may talk yourself into believing once again that you are unlovable or unacceptable, with such a painful, messy past. You could use this negative information and history for condemnation, instead of healing. That is why we must tell another person. We must realize that we are loved and accepted, even though we have been places and experienced things of which we are not proud.

In this Fifth Step you experience a spiritual, emotional, and often physical cleansing which lightens your load. As you share who you have been, and what you have experienced with another trusted person, you are reassured that nothing you have done makes you unlovable. Now someone knows the whole truth, and still loves you. It is remarkable!

A note of caution is appropriate here. When you choose someone to hear your Fifth Step, it is important to pick the least condemning, most loving, and accepting person you know. You might choose a therapist, sponsor, or spiritual person you trust. Choose someone who understands that you are digging into your past, in order to make your present and future better. This choice is yours, so make it in your best interest.

The Exact Nature of Our Wrongs. The fact that this part of the step is so specific will help two kinds of people; those who say, "I can't be specific, so I'll never really feel loved," and those who believe that they can own everybody else's wrongs, and avoid looking at their own choices. The first person needs to be specific in sharing her story because the purpose of sharing is not to shame her for her past. Shame can come from memories tied to specific episodes. We must talk about those specific episodes to relieve the shame associated with them. The second person needs to acknowledge her own shortcomings and "clean her own side of the street," not anyone else's, so that she too, can be freed from her own shame.

It's a recognized fact that you can't free anyone else from her shame. Each person has to work her own program of recovery, in order to have the kind of happy and fulfilling life we are all capable of experiencing.

6

WERE ENTIRELY READY TO HAVE GOD REMOVE ALL THESE DEFECTS OF CHARACTER.

Were Entirely Ready. As you move from Step One through Step Five, you discover a process through which you recognize powerlessness, find a God of your understanding, go inside yourself by writing an inventory, and let someone else know who you really are. The very core of the program is in the first five steps. By working these steps, you have learned to "trust God and clean house."

Now that you have cleaned house, you must learn how to maintain your new surroundings. It is one process to clean a dirty house, whether you got it dirty yourself, or just inherited all the mess. It is another thing entirely to make sure that it never gets dirty again. That is what Step Six and the following steps are all about—preventative maintenance.

You start by being ready. This simply means that you are 100% ready to look at the damage that was done by all that trash and you evaluate what you can throw away. You might be quite attached to some of that stuff. Even though it doesn't work any longer, you hesitate to give it up. Someday, some of those old behaviors might come in handy, you keep thinking. You forget that each time you try old behavior it causes great pain. "Were entirely ready" indicates that you are finally tired of the pain. You finally realize that changing is not as frightening as staying the same.

To Have God. Having God in our lives is so significant for partners of betrayal trauma. Here, in Step Six, they are reminded that they (like everyone) are blessed by having a relationship with God. They are beginning to believe that

God does want the best for them. God also wants their lives to express this new way of feeling and believing about themselves. God is willing to work with you, as you continue your efforts at recovery.

Remove All. This sounds like an unrealistic, maybe even painful statement, at least from a human standpoint. Remove indicates loss. Partners of betrayal trauma have certainly experienced loss in their lives, but to lose or remove all of their defects, how is this done?

Well, it isn't up to you to decide how, it's only up to you to be ready. Remember that earlier you recognized that you don't have a whole lot of power of your own. In Step Six you will rely on God to have the power to change you.

Defects of Character. As you consider the term "defects of character" you might be thinking of some of the ways you have behaved in the past that didn't work very well. Go ahead, get a pencil and paper, and write down what comes to mind. Reviewing your inventory should give you a good idea of things about your character you might want to change.

For example, perhaps the way you express your anger indicates a defect of character. Things you might want to change include the way you control and try to manipulate your spouse or children, or perhaps the way you pout to get your own way, or isolate yourself from others, or run away from responsibility. It is important to be honest when you list these defects, because the ones you hold on to will keep you stuck in old patterns and you will continue to attract unhealthy people into your life, especially in intimate relationships.

It is the experience of recovering partners that as you become more healthy and honest you will gravitate toward more healthy and honest people, and you will be better equipped to determine who is unhealthy. Understanding this should motivate you to really look at your defects of character and be 100% willing to ask God to remove them. This is the real release that prevents the dust and trash from resettling in your house.

7

HUMBLY ASKED HIM TO REMOVE OUR SHORTCOMINGS.

Humbly. Many people struggle with the word humble, having been humiliated (time and again), by his choice to betray you. Humility is not the same as humiliation, although you may feel something like humiliation when you see the devastation in your own life and the lives of those around you, caused by your defects of character. Humility, in this case, means recognizing your true humanity. Step Seven shows you the manner with which you should approach God. Humility means knowing that you don't have the power to change yourself, but God does. You come into God's presence with a humble heart, but with hope as well. And, as you ask, you shall receive. As long as you don't have preconceived ideas of just how, and when, God will remove your defects of character.

Asked God. Humility requires that we ask, not tell God anything. By now, perhaps you have come to believe that God really does want the best for you and wants you to be free of your defects of character. God wants you to feel good about yourself and to be attracted to healthy people. You are asking, in a sense, to do God's will.

To Remove Our Shortcomings. In Step Six you became ready. Now you push the "Go" button, asking God to take away your defects of character, or shortcomings. It would be nice if it happened all at once, but again, you will experience it as a process. In this process, God will be with you throughout your life, removing your shortcomings as you continue to identify them when they surface, as long as you are willing to ask for help.

For some partners, this Step comes easy. For others, it is very hard, especially if you are still rationalizing, still defending, still gripping your defense mechanisms. In that case, Step Seven can be a painful experience. As someone once said in a meeting, "There was never anything I let go of, that didn't have claw marks all over it, including my defects of character."

You can trust that if you ask, God will remove your defects of character, no matter how much you resist. If you decide to hold on to them, you will be fighting a losing battle. It is at this point that you will really need your support group. They will give you valuable feedback about any shortcomings they see you holding on to. If you aren't sure, ask questions. They will also give you support as you try new behaviors, in place of the old ones that kept you so unhappy. Allow them to support you in this growth process.

8

MADE A LIST OF ALL PERSONS WE HAD HARMED, AND BECAME WILLING TO MAKE AMENDS TO THEM ALL.

Made A List. You probably don't have any problem shopping for groceries if you've made a list. The most efficient way to shop is to have a written list (instead of just mental notes), because otherwise you are likely to get home and find you have forgotten some essential items. There is a saying in Alcoholics Anonymous that you should be "fearless and thorough from the very start." This is true in Step Eight. Again, take a pencil and paper in hand and after looking at your inventory make a list of all the people you have harmed. This list should include yourself, as well as others, and can also include what damage was done and the person's name.

Of All Persons. Here again is that sometimes scary word "all." All means every single one. You are, once again, being challenged to be honest. To the degree that you can be honest in making this list, you have hope for new relationships with important people in your life.

We Had Harmed. It takes an honest person to look at her life and see the people she has harmed. It is often easier to see how you have been harmed by others. In Steps Four and Five, you looked at how you have been hurt by trusted people in your life, how you have been traumatized, how you have been emotionally abandoned, and how you have suffered. But if all you look at is how you have been harmed, you are only halfway healed.

Just as it can be painful for a recovering alcoholic to see how his drinking damaged those around him, so it can be painful for the recovering partner to realize what she has done to hurt others. For many partners, it is much more comfortable to be the victim. As a matter of fact, they have often been the victim of their own behaviors, of their own past, and even of recent relationships. But past victimization by others, just makes it that much more difficult for these people to realize that they have actually harmed other people. The "me acting out" behavior is just the start of this list. The harm can be very subtle. You need to really search your mind and heart, in order to complete your healing.

And Became Willing. The past tense here reminds you (one more time), that the hard work demanded in the previous steps is survivable. Partners have worked their way through these steps before and have found peace and happiness on the other side. It also indicates a process. Recovery doesn't just happen overnight. Becoming willing takes time for everyone, especially if they are holding on to a victim status.

To Make Amends. What does it mean to make amends? For partners, or anyone in recovery for that matter, to make amends means to acknowledge the wrong they have done and be willing to be different. You stop blaming the other person to justify your own behavior. You stop rationalizing and defending yourself. You stop avoiding responsibility. You continue to change in your relationships with yourself and others. You take full responsibility for what you have done, and to whom you have done it, at least on paper at this point, even if your wrong is less than their wrong.

To Them All. Here is that word "all" again. It seems to appear everywhere throughout the Twelve Steps. By now your list should include everyone who has in any way been harmed by your actions, or lack of actions. You should have found the willingness to be different with each person on that list, including yourself. No stone should be left unturned at this point, or you will still carry old guilt that will keep you stuck in old sick patterns of thinking and relating. With names, phone numbers, and accounts of damages in hand, you are ready to move on.

9

MADE DIRECT AMENDS TO SUCH PEOPLE WHEREVER POSSIBLE, EXCEPT WHEN TO DO SO WOULD INJURE THEM OR OTHERS.

Made Direct Amends. In Step Eight, you made your list. Now you go to the "grocery store." In Step Nine, you actually go to the people on your list and make direct amends to them for the inappropriate attitudes or behaviors you have had in the past that have affected them. Notice again that this step is written in the past tense. These steps were written in the late 1930s when the first members of Alcoholics Anonymous became sober. Working these steps, especially Step Nine, was something they had to do to maintain their sobriety, so they would not have to carry the pain, shame, or guilt of the past or present into their new sober lives.

They had to be honest with themselves. So, do you, as you go to each person on your list and ask them for their forgiveness. When you acknowledge how your behavior affected your relationships with them, you will find incredible freedom. Tremendous emotional weights are lifted, often relationships are restored as the result of working Step Nine. This is not a 100% guarantee, since some relationships will remain fractured. However, at least your side of the street will be clean.

You will begin to feel wholeness and happiness in your life, now that you have made the effort to vent completely, without expectations. This is a significant point: You do not make amends with the expectation that your friends or family will change their behavior. You do not make amends with the expectation that people will respond in any certain way. People may, in fact, respond when you make amends. However, it is by no means the motivation for you to do what you must to rid yourself from what you have been carrying for so long. Inflated expectations can cause you much pain because others are not always in the same place with their recovery that you are with yours. Many people do not choose a path of recovery at all. Your personal efforts and behavior, however, may challenge them into this kind of recovery at some point in the future.

It is not a given that the other person will ask forgiveness in return, even though they may have injured you much more than you have injured them. Your goal is to clean your own slate. You are not responsible for what others leave undone, nor can their shortcomings keep you from recovering and feeling good about yourself.

Except When to Do So Would Injure Them or Others. When you get to this point, you might be confused trying to determine if making amends will injure the person involved, or be detrimental to others, possibly innocent people. Such confusion is best resolved with the assistance of a group, sponsor, or therapist. Confusion is not to be used, however, as an excuse to not make any amends because you don't want to experience the pain or shame of admitting your past behavior.

What you must consider when admitting past behavior is whether or not your confession would so significantly damage the other person involved that you should not raise the issue with them. You can ask yourself, "Would this be damaging?" If you have a question, do not assume you have the answer. You could very possibly avoid an amend which could restore a relationship or hold on to an amend that will set you up for old behavior. Go over your list with a sponsor, support group, or therapist, if at all possible.

10

CONTINUED TO TAKE PERSONAL INVENTORY, AND WHEN WE WERE WRONG, PROMPTLY ADMITTED IT.

Continued. Here again you must deal with the maintenance of your newly clean house. You are not letting the dust fall. You are not letting the dirt collect or the garbage overflow in the can. Here you are in a process, as in Steps Four and

Five. Today, when you have been inappropriate or have violated anyone's boundaries (including your own), you don't have to wait five or ten years to make amends. You can do it as you go along.

To Take Personal Inventory. Taking a daily personal inventory is a process in which partners are able to look at each person in their life and see how they are interacting with them. They look at their attitudes toward others and honestly evaluate them. This is not done to the point where they are unable to enjoy interactions, but it is an honest evaluation of how they respond to peers, family, and in all other relationships. It it is also a reminder to focus on (or inventory) only their behavior, not anyone else's.

And When We Were Wrong, Promptly Admitted It. You will be wrong. This part of Step Ten says, "when," not, "if," you were wrong. Many partners have been wronged, but there will still be times when you will be wrong yourself. It is so important for the recovering person to stay free, and not enter into a place of guilt and shame, which can push you into some acting out behavior. So, in the maintenance of Step Ten, when you are wrong, you promptly admit it. Promptly is significant because it keeps you from holding on to the baggage, thinking for months about whether you were or weren't wrong. Promptly means admit it right now, right here. If you have been acting inappropriately, say, "I'm sorry. Forgive me, I'm acting inappropriately." It is as simple as that. Step Ten gives you a way to stay free from the bondage of guilt and shame. It keeps you humble, which often helps you to remain healthy.

11

SOUGHT THROUGH PRAYER AND MEDITATION TO IMPROVE OUR CONSCIOUS CONTACT WITH GOD AS WE UNDERSTOOD HIM, PRAYING ONLY FOR KNOWLEDGE OF HIS WILL FOR US AND THE POWER TO CARRY THAT OUT.

Sought Through Prayer and Meditation. This step not only tells you what you are doing, but it also tells you how to do it. You are seeking. You are looking to improve your relationship with God. This step tells you to do that through prayer and meditation. Prayer is verbal and sometimes internal communication with God. It is such a positive experience for the partner to become more aware of God in her life. This step lets you know that it is your responsibility. Seeking requires action on your part. You may have felt abandoned by God, since you put no real effort into trying to find out where He was. It has been said many times in meetings, "If you can't find God, guess who moved?" You move away from God. God never moves away from you. Seeking Him is all that it takes to find Him.

Meditation is a sometimes a deeper sense of prayer. Prayer is requesting, asking, and interacting with God. Meditation is listening and hearing God's voice. Many people experience rest and peace through meditation. When you meditate you are able to still the constant obsessive thinking that prevents you from hearing what God says about you—that you are significant, you are loved, and you deserve to be healthy. Meditate on God's character, on your personal relationship with Him, on Scripture, or recovery material you have, and allow these things to really sink in to your spirit. Be still and God will speak to you.

To Improve Our Conscious Contact with God. Most partners, like many people, have an unconscious contact with

God. They rely primarily on their own thinking and resources, and then connect with God only after they have thoroughly botched their lives. Step Eleven reminds you to keep God in your conscious mind. As you do so, you will be able to experience the power and love of God in a whole new way, as well as experience life in a whole new way. You will have a higher sense of purpose and joy. The result of this new awareness of God—on a moment to moment basis—is a better relationship with God. As with any relationship, efforts at improving the relationship requires time, energy, and some sort of communication. With time, you will find the method of communication that works best for you. There is no right or wrong way to do it. Just do it.

As We Understood Him. It is impossible for any one of us to totally understand God. Indeed, my understanding of God might not work for you and your understanding of God might not work for me. The beauty of the program is that you can begin to see evidence of God in other people. Remember this is not a job you undertake on your own. You come to a new understanding of God as you interact with the people in your support group, church, or other community of people seeking knowledge of God. As you listen, you will grow in your understanding through other people's experiences of God in their lives.

Praying Only for Knowledge of His Will for Us. By now, you are beginning to see the benefits of letting go, of surrendering your will. In Step Eleven, you are gently reminded that when you pray for God's will in your life, you are asking for the absolute best solution to whatever you are facing. So often, we push and push situations to turn out the way we want them to, only to find out that we got second, third, seventh, or tenth best. It is a positive thing to realize that you can trust God to have your best interest at heart. The people, places, and things you have given your will over to in the past did not have your best interest at heart. You now trust God enough to say, "Not my will, but thy will be done."

And the Power to Carry That Out. You pray for the knowledge of God's will, not just for the sake of having the information, but also for the power to carry it out. Having information without the willingness or power to carry it out, will not change anything. After prayer for the knowledge, you can now listen in meditation for God to tell you the things you need to do. Sometimes a path will open, sometimes God will bring to mind a defect of character that is getting in your way, and sometimes God will challenge you in the way you are behaving, through intuitive thoughts or feelings you may have. Often the power to make changes God wants to make comes through the people in your support group. The power can also come from seeing someone stuck in old behaviors. You can be motivated to change by seeing the consequences others are experiencing because of their unwillingness to act differently. Having asked for direction and listened for guidance, you can act with assurance knowing that if you are on the wrong track you will come to know it. And you always know that you're not alone.

12

HAVING HAD A SPIRITUAL AWAKENING AS THE RESULT OF THESE STEPS, WE TRIED TO CARRY THIS MESSAGE TO OTHERS AND TO PRACTICE THESE PRINCIPLES IN ALL OUR AFFAIRS.

Having Had A Spiritual Awakening as The Result of These Steps. It is no wonder that an individual who comes to the Twelve Steps, and in time admits to powerlessness, the frailty of being human, the need for a relationship with God, actively pursues that relationship, cleans house, makes amends, and maintains this behavior, has a spiritual awakening. This spiritual awakening is the purpose of working the Twelve Steps. It is an awakening in which the partner discovers she has worth and value, that she is loved by God, and can be loved by others, if she will believes in her "loveableness" and opens up her heart to let that love in.

This awakening to a spiritual connection with God can give partners the power to change their way of relating to themselves, and to the world. They can now see themselves as precious children of a loving God and treat themselves (and others) accordingly.

We Tried to Carry This Message to Others. In the beginning of Alcoholics Anonymous, it was not a matter of an alcoholic seeking advice and support from someone who was sober. It was the recovering alcoholic who sought out the active drinker. Bill W., the cofounder of AA, knew that if he couldn't share what he had discovered about his relationship with God and its importance to his sobriety, he wouldn't be able to stay sober. This is true for partners of betrayal trauma, too. As they progress in their recovery, and become less absorbed in their own pain, they will begin to see opportunities to share their experiences, strength, and hope with other partners. As you share your life with other women who are suffering from the same low self-esteem, dependency or independency problems, and lack of boundaries you experienced, you are reminded of the miracle of recovery in your own life. Without constant reminders, you are likely to forget where your strength and health came from and become complacent.

One of the truest sayings around recovery groups is, "You can't keep it, if you don't give it away." The door to recovery is opened to you, because others passed this way before. It is your joy, as well as your responsibility, to keep the door open for those who follow you and to lead them to the door if they can't find it. It is the only way to ensure freedom for all.

And to Practice These Principles in All Our Affairs. Here is the most practical part of the Twelve Steps. Take what you have learned and keep doing it every day. Practice admitting your powerlessness over the problems in your life. Practice acknowledging God's ability to run your life and keep you from practicing old behaviors. Practice new thinking and behavior skills. Practice prayer and meditation. Like the athlete who must exercise daily to stay in shape, you need to practice daily the new skills you have learned, so you can stay in good emotional and spiritual shape. It took many years of practicing old behaviors for you to end up with low self-esteem and a lack of boundaries. It will take practice to become the new person you want to be. But it is possible!

Congratulations to all who embark on this journey of the Twelve Steps. These steps, when followed, are a tried and true path toward healing from the effects of betrayal trauma. You may not have caused the pain, but you are the one now responsible to heal your pain. The partners I have counseled, that are most successful in this healing process, are those who actively worked the Twelve Steps. In addition to the vital attendance and involvement in Twelve Step recovery, many partners benefit greatly from professional therapy.

"YOU MAY NOT HAVE CAUSED THE PAIN, BUT YOU ARE THE ONE NOW RESPONSIBLE TO HEAL YOUR PAIN."

12

Finding A Counselor

Partners of betrayal trauma have been misunderstood, mislabeled, silenced, blamed, and even injured by therapists. I have cleaned up many bizarre things therapists have done and said to women.

I want to spend a little time explaining a few things that are sad realities in the counseling community today. First, I will look at credibility, then I will discuss training that may be beneficial for you to participate in.

I have personally Googled sex addiction help and sex addiction counselors or therapists in several major cities. What I found is that 90% (yes that's right 90%) have no training or certification in sex addiction. You wouldn't go to a doctor that advertises they treat a specific condition, if you found out the doctor was never trained to treat this condition, would you?

To take it a step further, many women and men who may be certified to treat sex addiction have almost no specialized training in partner issues, especially from this perspective at all. I say this because you are a partner of infidelity, sex addiction, or intimacy anorexia. Many sex addiction therapists also don't have any understanding of intimacy anorexia.

That is why any therapist I work with in my counseling center (even interns) have gone through training from the American Association for Sex Addiction Therapy (AASAT) for all three conditions: sex addiction, partners of sex addicts (which include specific DVD's on Partner Betrayal Trauma), and intimacy anorexia.

You also deserve to know if the therapist is a recovering sex addict, intimacy anorexic, or a partner in recovery. If they are, they can have great empathy. However, you want to make sure they are clean as well.

I remember a while back when I was interviewing potential private practice male therapists to help us at Heart to Heart Counseling Center. I told them my clients have been trained to ask them when was the last time you masturbated or viewed pornography. All, but one of the male therapists, was currently acting out regularly. This is sad enough, but none of them wanted to heal, and none attended our free groups. These therapists continued to practice with active sex addiction. I have had therapists who claim to be "partner" experts with no recovery experience that promote no sex for years to their female clients.

You are visiting the wrong office if your therapist can't be honest about their own recovery, if they are promoting themselves as a recovery person. On my wall, by my bookcase is a copy of my polygraph verifying my current 33 years of sexual sobriety.

Also, be aware of the following attitudes and beliefs about helping you as a partner. These include the therapist that tells you they will decide when he discloses to you. I know women who trusted their therapist and two years later their husband still wasn't ready. Protecting the addict keeps him in shame and you with absolutely needless anxiety. If they need a week or two to get the facts straight, then maybe. However, during our Intensives we do most of our polygraphs on Monday. He knows the general facts and he knows if he is actually lying about those facts.

If a therapist "doesn't believe" in polygraphs, you're in the wrong office. You have been lied to (often for years or decades), and are you supposed to just believe your husband or significant other?

"IF A THERAPIST 'DOESN'T BELIEVE' IN POLYGRAPHS, YOU'RE IN THE WRONG OFFICE."

Even when a man knows he is taking a polygraph in my office, half will lie to me and their wife, knowing minutes later the polygraph will reveal the truth. Addicts lie and that keeps them in shame. Countless men have thanked me because the polygraph helped them stop lying and helped them to stay sober.

Disclosure without a polygraph can be quite incomplete. When I say disclosure, I mean general disclosure. Specifics like positions and clothing are not polygraph disclosures. If a therapist tells you that you can't have sex you are in the wrong place. You haven't had a voice and now the therapist is taking your voice and sexual power. If your husband or significant other is present with you during sex (eyes open, lights on, with nurturing conversation), he is bonding to you and not acting out. I never bought into forced abstinence.

I clearly honor a woman who isn't playing games and needs a season to heal. That women sees a therapist and actually works on her healing. Recovery takes time and is complex involving grief, anger, bargaining, and so much more. I want you to get the best help possible. You can always talk to one of the therapists at our office at (719) 278-3708. You can also accelerate your healing by doing a 3 -or 5-Day Intensive with a therapist who has years of experience in my office.

In addition to the vital attendance and involvement in Twelve Step recovery, many partners benefit greatly from professional therapy.

"What? Am I in need of therapy, too?" Does the idea of therapy frighten you? A general discussion of the types of therapy available might help you decide if therapy is for you.

Like medical or financial fields, the mental health field has various levels of professionally trained people. These professionals have a wide variety of philosophies and training perspective that meet the different needs partners have.

<u>Partner Recovery Therapist</u>

A Partner Recovery Therapist (PRT) is someone who is a licensed Masters level counselor or psychologist. This person is highly trained in partner issues and recovery. The PRT will also be the first group of therapists to have been offered the Partner Betrayal Trauma Training DVDs that will be a part of all future PRTs.

This therapist accepts the core values of partner recovery. They go through over 30 hours of specific training on partner recovery. They also go through direct supervision with me, not someone else.

If you need to find someone with this distinctive training,

go to www.aasat.org. If there is no one in your area, call my office for a phone session with a PRT.

There are other companies who train people in counseling partners; however, each has different beliefs. Other companies may not have the information specifically on the partner betrayal trauma model you have been exposed to in this book.

Partner Recovery Coach

A partner recovery coach has become an acceptable person to help someone grow in any area of life. A coach is generally a person like you, who has experienced firsthand what it's like to be a partner of betrayal trauma. Some of their husbands did recovery, some failed to do recovery.

These coaches go through an approved coaching program. They also go through the partners training program DVDs through the American Association for Sex Addiction Therapy (AASAT). Coaches also receive six months of supervision with me, or someone directly trained by me.

A coach's approach and training focuses more on the present and moving forward. Whereas, counselors focuses on the present, as well as past issues (such as family of origin and sex abuse) while moving you forward.

I have trained several partners who became coaches and they can be very helpful. Again, you must verify they are actually trained. As we have learned in this book, each women's journey is unique. If a coach has no training, they are limited to their own experience and opinions.

If they are specifically trained for partners in recovery, this person can be helpful. If not, you are rolling the dice on what you can learn from a coach, or any other professional for that matter.

Psychiatrist

Psychiatrists are medical doctors. They attend several years of medical school and are trained to look at biological reasons for problems with the human being. They are also trained on the use of medications that influence the chemistry of the brain. This professional can be a valuable help or support to the partner of betrayal trauma who has previously been diagnosed with depression, bipolar disorder, or other problems that requires the supervision of a medical doctor. They can prescribe medication you might need to feel better, such as antidepressant medication.

If the psychiatrist has addiction training (or exposure to workshops dealing with the effects of sexual addiction), they may be of some help to you as you work through your recovery. Some psychiatrists may also help address thyroid or hormone control levels and other physical symptoms from the impact of partner betrayal trauma.

Psychologist

A psychologist is quite different from a psychiatrist, although they are often confused as they both have the designation of doctor. Psychologists receive doctorates in philosophy (PhD), education (EdD), or psychology (PsyD), but they are not medical doctors. They have not attended and graduated from medical school. They are not licensed physicians. Therefore, they cannot prescribe medication (in most cases). Psychologists spend their educational training looking at the cognitive, or thinking aspects of the human being, such as IQ, reading and math levels, psychological testing, and the like. They are often trained to do individual, group, and marital therapy.

A psychologist, with a doctorate in psychology, can be helpful to the partner betrayal trauma client, especially if the psychologist has experience working with sex addicts and their partners. A psychologist can be of help in providing therapy to a partner, particularly if the partner is experiencing a psychological problem, such as depression, suicidal thoughts, or a compulsive eating, sleeping, or alcohol disorder. Often these survival mechanisms respond well to treatment under the care of a trained and licensed psychologist.

Licensed Professional Counselor

The Licensed Professional Counselor (LPC) usually has either master's level training, or PhD level training with expertise in counseling or another field, (i.e., sociology or anthropology.) They acquire a counselor's license by taking certain counseling classes. A master's degree is the minimum required for the LPC in most states. The master's level professional may also have a degree in other areas than counseling such as a MEd (Master of Education). They take a prescribed number of classes in counseling (during or after completing a graduate degree program) to acquire a professional license from the state they practice in. This is something to note in your initial interview with a Licensed Professional Counselor. You should ask about their background since some states do not require a degree in counseling for licensure. It is important for partners of betrayal trauma to know this information before seeking help for their own issues, or for the issues regarding their family, marriage, or children.

The master's level LPC, much like a psychologist, can be a great resource for a partner of betrayal trauma as she deals with family and individual problems. A LPC is usually able to identify and deal with depression, obsessive compulsive disorders, addictive disorders, codependency, and other issues.

LPCs (like psychiatrists and psychologists) have ongoing training and, in most states, will have a more reasonable fee structure for those seeking counseling. In finding a Licensed Professional Counselor, ask how many years they have been practicing, and review the "Questions to Ask" section at the end of this chapter, to determine the counselor's experience with treating partners.

Social Worker

Social workers will have either a bachelor's (BSW), master's (MSSW), or doctorate (DSW or PhD). They may have several levels of certification which differ from state to state. They may be a certified social worker (CSW) or licensed clinical social worker (LCSW), depending on their training and experience. Their training is mostly from a social perspective. Seeing issues from a social perspective is beneficial, and can be helpful, but unless specific training is given to the social worker in the field of addictions, there may be limits as to how helpful this professional can be.

However, if there is a need for social services for the family, or for the sex addict in finding places for residential treatment, a social worker can usually be quite resourceful. In some states the social worker is much like a Licensed Professional Counselor, as they provide individual, group, or family therapy. In other states and situations, they may do social histories and things of that nature. In finding a social worker, you will need to find out what educational training and experience they have had. You may find that this will be a very beneficial relationship to you, as you seek help, for either your own issues, or those of your family. Again, refer to the "Questions to Ask" section at the end of this chapter for further information.

Pastoral Counselor

Pastoral counseling is also available in many areas. Pastoral counselors include people who have professional degrees in counseling from an accredited seminary or institution. They may have a doctorate (PhD), or a master's degree. Pastors of local congregations would be included in this category. Although most pastors minimally have a bachelor's level education, some may have no formal education at all. Such counselors can be significantly helpful to those who have strong church or religious background. Pastoral counselors can be very helpful in your recovery, because spiritual development is a significant part of recovery for the whole person.

Strengths of a pastoral counselor would include spiritual training, coupled with professional experience and professional training in the fields of addictions, or counseling and psychological training. With such training, a pastoral counselor could be of the utmost benefit.

Some possible weaknesses of the pastoral counselor might be a lack of training or skill in some areas. The pastor who has had no training in counseling, may be of brief support to the partner of betrayal trauma, but might not be as beneficial in resolving personal issues, or identifying other psychological problems that you might have. Pastors are usually not trained counselors but they can be a great support to the partner of betrayal trauma in the recovery process.

The pastoral counselor, like all other professionals discussed, should be asked the appropriate questions from the "Questions to Ask" section. This is very important. Often, their understanding of addictions and sexual issues can influence how therapeutic their services can be.

Christian Counseling

Christian counseling is another form of counseling which is readily available in larger cities, as well in some smaller communities. Christian counseling is not exactly the same thing as pastoral counseling. Many Christian counselors do not hold pastoral positions, nor will they have education or training on professional pastoral counseling.

A Christian counselor is often professionally trained in the theory of counseling, psychology, and human development. These counselors can be master's or doctoral level trained professionals, but the training that the counselor receives can vary widely. It is wise to check the Christian counselor's training prior to engaging in any therapeutic relationship.

There is a specific benefit in having a Christian counselor for those who embrace the Christian faith. They can be a great source of help, especially if they are able to integrate biblical truths and understanding into the healing process. They can be very supportive and encouraging to the personal development of the partner, as well as facilitating growth for the entire family. Again, ask the questions relating to training and expertise in the area of being a partner of betrayal trauma. Just because they are a Christian does not guarantee they understand, or successfully treat the effects of partner betrayal trauma.

Certified Alcohol and Drug Addiction Counselors or Licensed Chemical Dependency Counselor

Certified alcohol and drug addiction counselors (CADAC) and licensed chemical dependency counselors (LCDC) are available in most areas, although their designations may differ from state to state. These are counselors with a variety of training backgrounds.

They may have PhD, master's, or bachelor's degrees, or may have no formal education whatsoever. Again, the training of an individual counselor is very significant. This cannot be stressed more than in the field of alcohol and drug addictions. In some states, individuals recovering from alcoholism or drug addiction, who want to enter the helping profession, find that such certification is the easiest way into this field. They do have a valid experience and understanding of the addiction process, as well as understanding of the recovery process. However, caution must be used, in that recovering people often have multiple addiction problems. This is something to be noted when interviewing an addiction counselor. In addition, it is important to ask how they have integrated a Twelve Step philosophy into their own lives. Unless the counselor has completed at least Step Four or Five and has begun the process of making amends, their perceptions might still be clouded by guilt and shame, and the counselor might not be able to facilitate the growth you need in your life.

Addiction counselors do have some strengths, however. They are often trained in family systems theory. They are familiar with the dynamics of addiction and usually come from a Twelve Step perspective. Often these counselors are found working in alcohol and drug addiction treatment centers. Sometimes they share an office with a psychiatrist, psychologist, or master's level counselor. They are often supervised in their work by a degreed professional. You can ask if their case load is being supervised, and by whom, and what that supervision process entails. This is important, because some supervisors (due to time constraints), will not review each case thoroughly. Another benefit to an addiction counselor, is that they would be aware of recovery groups in your area and the importance of support groups.

Marriage and Family Counselor

Marriage and family counselors can have a variety of degrees or education. They may have a PhD or a master's degree in marriage and family counseling. For partners, this may or may not be helpful, depending on the situation. If you are in a marriage, or a committed relationship, this type of counselor can be very beneficial.

Marriage and family counselors come from a family systems approach, taking into consideration the needs of the entire family, not just the needs of one person. Also, they will be highly attuned to how each family member processes problems, and how the family members interact with each other.

For example, in some addiction systems, the addict is the one who is perceived as needing help, the wife is the one who is strong and "helps" the addict, while the children are her supporters (her cheerleaders in helping dad). From a systems approach, a counselor might observe this family dysfunction and point out, "dad appears to be sick, so that mom can be a helper to him." Mom now needs to give up the helper role and establish her own identity and boundaries, so if dad recovers, the family doesn't need somebody else to be sick (i.e., the children, or mother herself).

Marriage and family counselors are highly astute in these matters and can be beneficial to the partner of betrayal trauma, as well as to the family as a whole. Refer to the "Questions to Ask" section to determine what training and experience this counselor has in addictions (in general) and in sexual addiction (specifically) as well as partner betrayal trauma recovery.

It is appropriate to interview the professional you are considering as a therapist. Every addict has a different history, which could create possible conflicts with certain professionals due to their past experiences. Also, the various professionals discussed here represent a continuum of care. At one point in your recovery, you might find one type of professional more helpful than another. Many practices include several types of therapists and are able to treat partners of betrayal trauma from what is known as a multi-disciplinary approach.

In interviewing a potential counselor (or other professional), consider the following list of questions.

Questions to Ask

- Do you have experience working with partners of betrayal trauma from sex addiction, infidelity, or intimacy anorexia?
- How many partners of betrayal trauma have you counseled in the last two months?
- Do you have training to do therapy with people with addictions and their families? (State or Board certification)
- Are you a recovering person working a Twelve Step program?
- What books have you read on partners, sex addiction, infidelity, or intimacy anorexia?
- Do you have specific training to deal with (if these issues apply to you), rape victims, survivors of child sexual abuse, incest, or other trauma?

Telephone Counseling

The current number of professionals who are successful in treating partners of betrayal trauma, partners of sex addicts, infidelity, or intimacy anorexia can be limited, even in the larger metropolitan areas.

Heart to Heart Counseling Center has established telephone counseling for the partner of betrayal trauma, the addict, unfaithful spouse, or for couple counseling.

We have seen the same success rates for clients using telephone counseling as those who come into the office. More information can be found in the Appendix on this service. This form of counseling is especially helpful for those who travel quite a bit, because they can call in for their appointment from anywhere, and speak to the same counselor each week. Telephone counseling is also helpful to those who feel that confidentiality is of utmost importance. We see many physicians, lawyers, ministers, businessmen, and students who don't want to run into their counselor at the grocery store. They also don't have to walk into the counselor's office where they may be seen by someone they may know. Some like it because they don't have to find a babysitter to go to an appointment.

For whatever reason, using the phone for counseling has been very successful for the recovery process. These counselors may also have telephone groups you can be a part of. In these groups you work through the *Partner Betrayal Trauma Workbook* as well as other partner materials. You will also have a team of women you can call during the week.

3- and 5-Day Intensives

Three or Five Day Intensives are offered out of our offices in Colorado Springs, Colorado. We offer specific Intensives just for partners of betrayal trauma. We also have Intensives for Couples. Incredible growth and accelerated recovery can often happen for couples during this 3- or 5-day period. Three sessions are scheduled for couples each day. This is a great way to get a lot of recovery work done in a very short amount of time. For more information, see information on 3- and 5-Day Intensives in the Appendix, email Heart to Heart Counseling Center (heart2heart@xc.org), or call (719)278-3708.

During the healing process, many partners find it helpful to attend support groups to expedite their recovery. Groups can be a great asset to the partner experiencing betrayal trauma. I can't tell you how many partners over the years have told me how important their support group was during their healing process.

There are basically two types of groups for partners who want to heal from the effects of his sex addiction. The first of these is the traditional Twelve Step support group and the second group is what we call Partner Groups.

The traditional Twelve Step groups that exist are S-Anon, COSA, and COSLAA. Each of these groups are for partners of sex addicts and will have partners in them that understand (from one degree or another), where you have been and the hurt you are experiencing.

Some of these are very strong groups with good role models. The groups that reflect strength are those where they actually work their Twelve Steps individually and in group settings. Group members call one another for support during the week and utilize sponsor relationships. The partners in the group meetings stay focused on recovery. A strong Twelve Step group, regardless of which group it is, will help partners tremendously during recovery.

The type of Twelve Step groups to be wary of are characterized by these behaviors:

1. Not actively working the Twelve Steps individually, or as a group

2. Meetings feel like male bashing sessions, instead of focusing on partner issues

3. Group members do not have sponsors

4. The phone does not seem to be used by the group members

5. There is no mention of partners acting out, or slips, during meetings

These groups may mean well, but long-term, these behaviors allow you to stay in the problem instead of moving toward the solution. In almost any Twelve Step group, you will find a few members who are really working the program. Find the winners and stay with them. Even in the worst of groups, you can still try to do your own work.

I have seen transformation happen in the lives of partners as they attend Twelve Step support groups. I believe these groups can be of great help for you in your recovery process. The contact information for these groups is located in the Appendix of this book or call our office at (719) 278-3708.

The second type of group is what we call Partner Groups. There are some major differences between a Partner Group and a traditional Twelve Step Group. The first major difference is that you do not have to be codependent to be a member of the Partner Group. You can be healthy, or you can be unhealthy, due to the damage of his sex addiction, or previous life wounds. The second major difference is that this is a working group. All members of the group are expected to report in to the group as you complete exercises from the *Partner's Recovery Guide: 100 Empowering Exercises* and *Beyond Love: Twelve Step Guide for Partners, Married and Alone: Healing Exercises for Spouses* and *Married and Alone: The Twelve Step Guide*, or the *Partner Betrayal Trauma: Workbook* and *Partner Betrayal Trauma: Twelve Step Guide.*

The first part of a Partner Group is checking in. "Hi. This is Barbara. I am a partner of a sex addict. This week I have completed exercises #34 through #37 in the *Partner's Recovery Guide*, and I am working on Step Three in *Beyond Love*." This creates positive momentum in the group.

The person who wants to stay in the problem will be obvious to the rest of the group and even to herself, because of her lack of work. The people who do the work naturally become the leaders, instead of the strongest personality taking over. The group sessions for the Partner Groups are basically in three sections:

1. Checking in on your progress

2. A recovery topic given by the chairperson for group discussion

3. Small group check-ins.

The topic session is a time (approximately 30 minutes), when the group discusses a recovery topic. For the small group check-ins, two or three partners pair off and they talk about how they really are doing, and what is going on in their lives. This way each member gets to share fully how it is going, and receives feedback from the other one or two members of the group. This type of small group allows everyone to have time, instead of one partner who is in the most pain dominating the group time. This seems to work really well and helps the group meet each partner's needs. During this small group check-in, the person who is sharing can ask for feedback, and receive the strength and hope she needs, along with some positive tips from others.

If there is not a Partner Group in your local area, feel free to start one. You don't need to be a professional, just be willing to be available. If you call our office, we can direct you to the groups we know about. If there isn't one in your area, you might need to be the one to start one. If you do start a Partner Group, please notify our office. If you want us to put it in our newsletter (via e-mail) that goes out weekly to thousands of partners, we may be able to do this as well. For more information call (719) 278-3708 or e-mail us at heart-2heart@xc.org.

Now I also realize that some of you reading this book are quite a distance away from a major metropolitan area. The Internet is growing in its resources to partners of betrayal trauma. On our website we have links to online support groups on our links page at www.sexaddict.com.

No matter what kind of group you participate in, I believe a group of some type is definitely the way to expedite your healing from partner betrayal trauma. The partners in these groups have been where you are, and they can help you along in your recovery journey.

"NO MATTER WHAT KIND OF GROUP YOU PARTICIPATE IN, I BELIEVE A GROUP OF SOME TYPE IS DEFINITELY THE WAY TO EXPEDITE YOUR HEALING FROM PARTNER BETRAYAL TRAUMA."

Conclusion

You and I have traveled quite a road together. I have walked with many women who were traumatized. I have seen many of these women choose to trust again, and grow into amazing women regardless of his decisions.

I hope you have felt heard, validated, and understood. Although you have been betrayed, that betrayal has caused a unique trauma that can become so deep, words can't adequately describe your experience.

You are unique. Your trauma is unique and so your journey to healing will also be uniquely yours. I encourage you to engage other wounded heroes like yourself in groups and get help with trained professionals. Begin working on the *Partner Betrayal Trauma: Workbook* and the *Partner Betrayal Trauma: Step Guide*

We at Heart to Heart Counseling Center have loved serving many brave, good-hearted women like yourself compassionately and effectively. You can take the colors of your trauma and paint a picture of your life into the picture you desire!

Appendix

Feelings Exercise

1. I feel (put feeling word here) when (put a present situation).
2. I first remember feeling (put the same feeling word here) when (explain earliest occurrence of this feeling).

Guideline #1: No Examples about Each Other Guideline #2: Maintain Eye Contact Guideline #3: No Feedback

Abandoned
Abused
Aching
Accepted
Accused
Accepting
Admired
Adored
Adventurous
Affectionate
Agony
Alienated
Aloof
Aggravated
Agreeable
Aggressive
Alive
Alone
Alluring
Amazed
Amused
Angry
Anguished
Annoyed
Anxious
Apart
Apathetic
Apologetic
Appreciated
Appreciative
Apprehensive
Appropriate
Approved
Argumentative
Aroused
Astonished
Assertive
Attached
Attacked

Attentive
Attractive
Aware
Awestruck
Badgered
Baited
Bashful
Battered
Beaten
Beautiful
Belligerent
Belittled
Bereaved
Betrayed
Bewildered
Blamed
Blaming
Bonded
Bored
Bothered
Brave
Breathless
Bristling
Broken-up
Bruised
Bubbly
Burdened
Burned
Callous
Calm
Capable
Captivated
Carefree
Careful
Careless
Caring
Cautious
Certain
Chased

Cheated
Cheerful
Childlike
Choked Up
Close
Cold
Comfortable
Comforted
Competent
Competitive
Complacent
Complete
Confident
Confused
Considerate
Consumed
Content
Cool
Courageous
Courteous
Coy
Crabby
Cranky
Crazy
Creative
Critical
Criticized
Cross
Crushed
Cuddly
Curious
Cut
Damned
Dangerous
Daring
Dead
Deceived
Deceptive
Defensive

Delicate
Delighted
Demeaned
Demoralized
Dependent
Depressed
Deprived
Deserted
Desirable
Desired
Despair
Despondent
Destroyed
Different
Dirty
Disenchanted
Disgusted
Disinterested
Dispirited
Distressed
Distrustful
Distrusted
Disturbed
Dominated
Domineering
Doomed
Doubtful
Dreadful
Eager
Ecstatic
Edgy
Edified
Elated
Embarrassed
Empowered
Empty
Enraged
Enraptured
Enthusiastic

Enticed
Esteemed
Exasperated
Excited
Exhilarated
Exposed
Fake
Fascinated
Feisty
Ferocious
Foolish
Forced
Forceful
Forgiven
Forgotten
Free
Friendly
Frightened
Frustrated
Full
Funny
Furious
Gay
Generous
Grouchy
Grumpy
Hard
Harried
Hassled
Healthy
Helpful
Helpless
Hesitant
High
Hollow
Honest
Hopeful
Hopeless
Horrified

Hostile
Humiliated
Hurried
Hurt
Hyper
Ignorant
Joyous
Lively
Lonely
Loose
Lost
Loving
Low
Lucky
Lustful
Mad
Maudlin
Malicious
Mean
Miserable
Misunderstood
Moody
Morose
Mournful
Mystified
Nasty
Nervous
Nice
Numb
Nurtured
Nuts
Obsessed
Offended
Open
Ornery
Out of control
Overcome
Overjoyed
Overpowered
Overwhelmed
Pampered
Panicked
Paralyzed

Paranoid
Patient
Peaceful
Pensive
Perceptive
Perturbed
Phony
Pleasant
Pleased
Positive
Powerless
Present
Precious
Pressured
Pretty
Proud
Pulled apart
Put down
Puzzled
Quarrelsome
Queer
Quiet
Raped
Ravished
Ravishing
Real
Refreshed
Regretful
Rejected
Rejuvenated
Rejecting
Relaxed
Relieved
Remarkable
Remembered
Removed
Repulsed
Repulsive
Resentful
Resistant
Responsible
Responsive
Repressed
Respected

Restless
Revolved
Riled
Rotten
Ruined
Sad
Safe
Satiated
Satisfied
Scared
Scolded
Scorned
Scrutinized
Secure
Seduced
Seductive
Self-centered
Self-conscious
Selfish
Separated
Sensuous
Sexy
Shattered
Shocked
Shot down
Shy
Sickened
Silly
Sincere
Sinking
Smart
Smothered
Smug
Sneaky
Snowed
Soft
Solid
Solitary
Sorry
Spacey
Special
Spiteful
Spontaneous
Squelched

Starved
Stiff
Stimulated
Stifled
Strangled
Strong
Stubborn
Stuck
Stunned
Stupid
Subdued
Submissive
Successful
Suffocated
Sure
Sweet
Sympathy
Tainted
Tearful
Tender
Tense
Terrific
Terrified
Thrilled
Ticked
Tickled
Tight
Timid
Tired
Tolerant
Tormented
Torn
Tortured
Touched
Trapped
Tremendous
Tricked
Trusted
Trustful
Trusting
Ugly
Unacceptable
Unapproachable

Unaware
Uncertain
Uncomfortable
Under control
Understanding
Understood
Undesirable
Unfriendly
Ungrateful
Unified
Unhappy
Unimpressed
Unsafe
Unstable
Upset
Uptight
Used
Useful
Useless
Unworthy
Validated
Valuable
Valued
Victorious
Violated
Violent
Voluptuous
Vulnerable
Warm
Wary
Weak
Whipped
Whole
Wicked
Wild
Willing
Wiped out
Wishful
Withdrawn
Wonderful
Worried
Worthy

The Twelve Steps of Alcoholics Anonymous

Adapted for Partners Betrayed by their Spouse or Significant Other

1. We admitted we were powerless over the betrayal from our spouse/significant other—that our lives had become unmanageable.

2. Came to believe that a Power greater than ourselves could restore us to sanity.

3. Made a decision to turn our will and our lives over to the care of God as we understood Him.

4. Made a searching and fearless moral inventory of ourselves.

5. Admitted to God, to ourselves, and to another human being the exact nature of our wrongs.

6. Were entirely ready to have God remove all these defects of character.

7. Humbly asked Him to remove our shortcomings.

8. Made a list of all people we had harmed, and became willing to make amends to them all.

9. Made direct amends to such people wherever possible, except when to do so would injure them or others.

10. Continued to take personal inventory, and when we were wrong, promptly admitted it.

11. Sought through prayer and meditation to improve our conscious contact with God as we understood Him, praying only for knowledge of His will for us and the power to carry that out.

12. Having had a spiritual awakening as the result of these steps, we tried to carry this message to others, and to practice these principles in all our affairs.

NEW PRODUCTS

MOVING FORWARD

In this video, Dr. Doug Weiss uses his decades of experience helping women move forward after being divorced from their sexually addicted or intimacy anorexic husband to help you process your situation more effectively and intelligently.

DVD: $29.95

INDESTRUCTIBLE

The Indestructible video gives you a foundational understanding about your innate design as God's child. Addiction, betrayal, and abuse or neglected can all cause trials in our lives that can trigger feelings of worthlessness and defeat.

DVD: $29.00

SEX AFTER RECOVERY

Sex after Recovery will help you navigate a variety of issues including how to reclaim a healthy sexual life together. This DVD set will help you to reclaim and recover your sexuality both individually and with each other.

DVD: $59.95

NEW PRODUCTS

HEALING HER HEART AFTER RELAPSE

Relapse doesn't have to occur, but if it happens, knowing how to navigate it intelligently can make a huge difference in a marriage. Each relapse impacts the wife significantly. Every couple in recovery would do well to have these tools before a potential relapse.

DVD: $29.95

PAIN FOR LOVE

Pain For Love describes in detail one of the most insidious strategies of an intimacy anorexic with their spouse. This dynamic is experienced by many who are married to an intimacy anorexic. This paradigm can empower the spouse and help them stop participating in a pain for love dynamic in their marriage.

DVD: $29.95

SIN OF WITHHOLDING

This DVD is the first to address the Biblical foundation of the sin of withholding in believers' hearts. The practical application in marriage addressing Intimacy Anorexia is also interwoven in this revelational teaching on the Sin of Withholding. Once a believer is free of this sin, their walk with the Lord and their fruit towards others can increase expediently.

DVD: $49.95

WOMEN'S RECOVERY

Partners: Healing From His Addiction book is the latest in research of the affects on a woman who has lived with a sexual addict. The riveting statistics combined with personal stories of recovery make this a must read book for any woman in a relationship with a sex addict. This book gives you hope and a beginning plan for personal recovery.

BOOK: $14.95

PARTNER'S RECOVERY GUIDE

This is like therapy in a box for women who want to walk through the residual effects of being in a relationship with a sex addict.

WORKBOOK: $39.95

BEYOND LOVE

This is an interactive workbook that allows the partners of sex addicts to gain insight and strength through working the Twelve Steps.

STEP BOOK: $14.95

HE NEEDS TO CHANGE, DR. WEISS

He Needs To Change, Dr. Weiss DVD addresses the pain, trauma, and betrayal women experience because of their partner's sex addiction, betrayal, and/or intimacy anorexia.In this DVD, Dr. Weiss addresses the issue of change that he has explained to thousands of women in his office.

DVD: $29.95

UNSTUCK FOR PARTNERS

The *Unstuck* DVD is for every woman who has experienced the pain of their partner's sex addiction or intimacy anorexia and feels stuck, confused, frustrated and unable to move on. You didn't sign up for this and honestly, you don't get it! This DVD helps you "get it" so you can process the painful reality you are in and start to live again.

DVD: $29.95

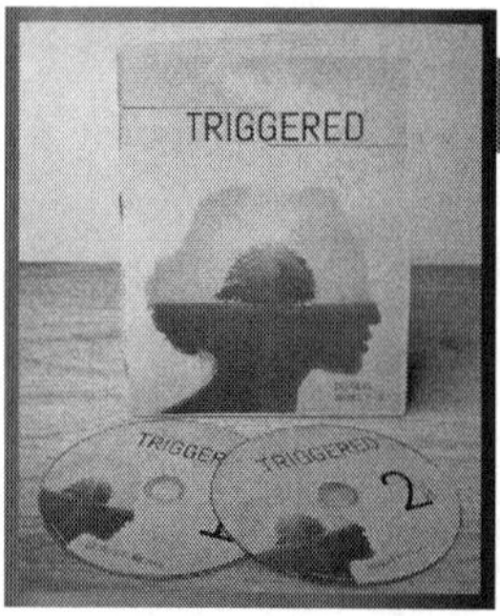

TRIGGERED

Triggers are normal for partners of sex addicts, but each woman's triggers are unique and must be navigated in different ways. This DVD can be a life-changing message which will validate your struggles to heal and help you face the challenges of being triggered after partner betrayal trauma.

DVD: $49.00

DISCLOSURE

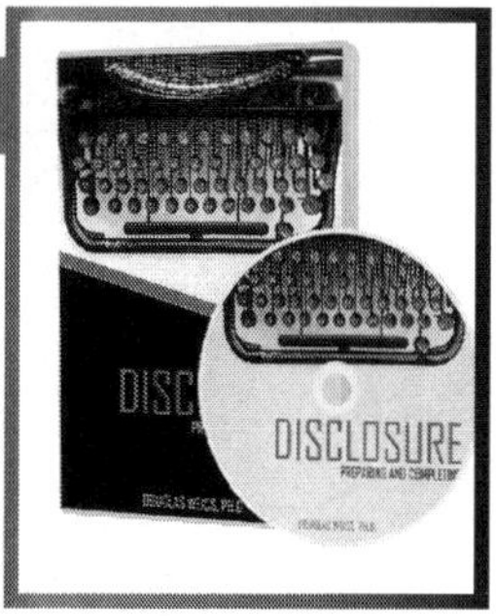

Disclosure is one of the most important topics in sexual addiction recovery. In this DVD, Dr. Weiss discusses the various types of disclosure. Each type of disclosure is for a specific purpose or person. This DVD can expedite the understanding of each of the significant processes of disclosure for the addict, the spouse and the marriage.

DVD: $39.95

PARTNER BETRAYAL TRAUMA

Partner Betrayal Trauma is real. Your pain and experience of betrayal has impacted all of your being and all of your relationships.

The book, DVD set, Workbook and Step guide were designed to help guide you thoughtfully through your own personal healing from the effects of being betrayed by your spouse or significant other. The pain and trauma of being betrayed, especially sexual betrayal, by a spouse or significant other is multidimensional and multifaceted. Your pain and trauma are real and these resources will help you in your journey of recovery from Partner Betrayal Trauma.

BOOK: $22.95 DVD: $65.95 WORKBOOK: $39.95 STEPBOOK: $14.95

INTIMACY ANOREXIA

This hidden addiction is destroying so many marriages today. In your hands is the first antidote for someone with intimacy anorexia to turn the pages on this addiction process. Excerpts from intimacy anorexics and their spouses help this book become clinically helpful and personal in its impact to communicate hope and healing for the intimacy anorexic and the marriage.

BOOK: $22.95
DVD: $69.95

INTIMACY ANOREXIA: THE WORKBOOK

This is like therapy in a box. Inside is 100 exercises that have already been proven helpful in treating intimacy anorexia.

WORKBOOK: $39.95

INTIMACY ANOREXIA: THE STEPS

This is the only twelve step workbook just for intimacy anorexia. Each step gives you progress in your healing from intimacy anorexia.

STEP BOOK: $14.95

MARRIED & ALONE

This is for the spouse of an intimacy anorexic. You feel disconnected, untouched and often unloved. You are not crazy and Dr. Weiss will help you to start a journey of recovery from living with a spouse with intimacy anorexia.

BOOK: $14.95
DVD: $49.95

MARRIED & ALONE: HEALING EXERCISES FOR SPOUSES

This is the first workbook to offer practical suggestions and techniques to better navigate through recovery from your spouse's Intimacy Anorexia.

WORKBOOK: $39.95

MARRIED & ALONE: THE TWELVE STEP GUIDE

This Twelve Step guide will help the spouse of an intimacy anorexic work through the Twelve Steps that many others have found to be helpful in their recovery.

STEP BOOK: $14.95

MEN'S RECOVERY

This book gives more current information than many professional counselors have today. In addition to informing sex addicts and their partners about sex addiction, it gives hope for recovery. The information provided in this book would cost hundreds of dollars in counseling hours to receive. Many have attested to successful recovery from this information alone.

BOOK: $22.95
CD: $35.00

101 FREEDOM EXERCISES

This is the best single resource for the Christian who desires to know what they need to do to get and stay free from sexual addiction. This book contains 101 exercises that have been proven to work.

WORKBOOK: $39.95

STEPS TO FREEDOM

This is a Christian approach to the Twelve Steps. This book will guide you through the 12 Steps of recovery that have been helpful for many addicted people. This book is specifically written for the person desiring recovery from sexual addiction.

STEP BOOK: $14.95

HELPING HER HEAL

The *Helping Her Heal* DVD is for the man who has disclosed his sexual addiction to his partner or spouse. This DVD offers practical tools for hearing her pain, navigating her grief and losses, discovering her expectations of you and the boundaries she may need to heal.

DVD: $69.95
DVD COMPANION GUIDE: $11.95

MARRIED AFTER ADDICTION

Addiction can have devastating effects on even good marriages. In this DVD you are intelligently guided through the journey you will experience if addiction is part of your marriage story. You will learn important information about the early and later stages of recovery for your marriage.

DVD: $29.95

SERIES FOR MEN

CLEAN

BOOK: $16.95
DVD: $29.95
JOURNAL: $16.95

Every Christian man is born into a sexual war. The enemy attacks the young, hoping to scar them permanently and leave them ruined. Your past is not enough to keep you from the enduringly clean life you want and deserve. This series can be used individually or in a small group setting.

LUST FREE LIVING

Every man can fight for and obtain a lust free lifestyle. Once you know how to stop lust, you will realize how weak lust really can be. God gace you the power to protect those you love from the ravages of lust for the rest of your life! It's time to take it back!

BOOK: $13.95
DVD: $23.95

MEN MAKE MEN

Dr. Weiss takes the listeners by the hand and step-by-step walks through the creative process God used to make every man into a man of God. This practical teaching on DVD combined with the Men Make Guidebook can revitalize the men in any home or local church.

DVD: $29.95
GUIDEBOOK: $11.95

MARRIAGE RESOURCES

LOVER SPOUSE

Lover Spouse helps you understand marriage from a Christ-centered perspective. Christian Marriages were designed to be different, passionate, fulfilling, and long-lasting. BOOK: $13.95

UPGRADE YOUR SEX LIFE

Upgrade Your Sex Life actually teaches you own unique sexual expression that you and your partner are pre-wired to enjoy.

BOOK: $16.95

SERVANT MARRIAGE

Servant Marriage book is a Revelation on God's Masterpiece of marriage. In these pages, you will walk with God as He creates the man, the woman and his masterpiece called marriage.

BOOK: $13.95

MARRIAGE MONDAYS

This is an eight week marriage training that actually gives you the skills to have a healthy and more vibrant marriage.

BOOK: $16.95

INTIMACY

This 100 Day guide can transform couples from any level of intimacy to a lifestyle of satiation with their spouse. BOOK: $11.95

MIRACLE OF MARRIAGE

God made your marriage to be an amazing and unique miracle. Dr. Weiss walks you through the creation and maintenance of your marriage. You will be exposed to a practical insights that can help make your marriage into God's original design.

DVD: $12.95

OTHER RESOURCES

WORTHY: EXERCISES & STEP BOOK

The *Worthy* Workbook and DVD, is designed for a 12 week study. Here is a path that anyone can take to get and stay worthy. Follow this path, and you too will make the journey from worthless to worthy just as others have.

DVD: $29.95
BOOK: $29.95

EMOTIONAL FITNESS

Everyone has an unlimited number of emotions, but few have been trained to identify, choose, communicate, and master them. More than a guide for gaining emotional fitness and mastery, in these pages you will find a pathway to a much more fulfilling life.

BOOK: $16.95

LETTERS TO MY DAUGHTER

A gift for your daugher as she enters college. *Letters to my Daughter* includes my daily letters to my daughter during her first year of college.

BOOK: $14.95

BORN FOR WAR

Born for War teaches practical tools to defeat these sexual landmines and offers scriptural truths that empower young men to desire successfulness in the war thrust upon them.

DVD: $29.95

PRINCES TAKE LONGER THAN FROGS

This 2 hour DVD helps single women ages 15-30, to successfully navigate through the season of dating.

DVD: $29.95

SUCCESSFULLY SINGLE

This 2 Disc DVD Series is definitely nothing you have heard before. Dr. Weiss charts new territory as to the why for sexual purity.

DVD: $29.95

COUNSELING

"Without the intensive, my marriage would have ended and I would not have known why. Now I am happier than ever and my marriage is bonded permanently."

COUNSELING SESSIONS

Couples are helped through critical phases of disclosure moving into the process of recovery, and rebuilding trust in relationships. We have helped many couples rebuild their relationship and grasp and implement the necessary skills for an intimate relationship.

Individual counseling offers a personal treatment plan for successful healing in your life. In just one session a counselor can help you understand how you became stuck and how to move toward freedom.

Partners of sex addicts need an advocate. Feelings of fear, hurt, anger, betrayal, and grief require a compassionate, effective response. We provide that expert guidance and direction. We have helped many partners heal through sessions that get them answers to their many questions including: "How can I trust him again?"

A counseling session today can begin your personal journey toward healing.

3 AND 5 DAY INTENSIVES

in Colorado Springs, Colorado are available for the following issues:

- Sexual Addiction Couple or Individual
- Partners of Sexual Addicts
- Victims of Sexual Abuse
- Teenage Children of Sex Addicts
- Marriage Intensives
- Intimacy Anorexia
- Adult Children of Sex Addicts

ATTENDEES OF INTENSIVES WILL RECEIVE:

- Personal attention from counselors who specialize in your area of need
- An understanding of how the addiction /anorexia and its consequences came into being
- Three appointments daily
- Daily assignments to increase the productiveness of these daily sessions
- Individuals get effective counseling to recover from the effects of sexual addiction, abuse and anorexia
- Addiction, abuse, anorexia issues are thoroughly addressed for couples and individuals. This includes the effects on the partner or family members of the addict, and how to rebuild intimacy toward a stronger relationship.